Multi-Agency Working the Early Years

Mar
Tel:

2 6 J

1 7 F

2

Tc

Education at SAGE

SAGE is a leading international publisher of journals, books, and electronic media for academic, educational, and professional markets.

Our education publishing includes:

- accessible and comprehensive texts for aspiring education professionals and practitioners looking to further their careers through continuing professional development

- inspirational advice and guidance for the classroom

- authoritative state of the art reference from the leading authors in the field

Find out more at: **www.sagepub.co.uk/education**

Multi-Agency Working in the Early Years: Challenges and Opportunities

Michael Gasper

Los Angeles | London | New Delhi
Singapore | Washington DC

First published 2010

Reprinted 2010

SAGE Publications Ltd
1 Oliver's Yard
55 City Road
London EC1Y 1SP

SAGE Publications Inc.
2455 Teller Road
Thousand Oaks, California 91320

SAGE Publications India Pvt Ltd
B 1/I 1 Mohan Cooperative Industrial Area
Mathura Road
New Delhi 110 044

SAGE Publications Asia-Pacific Pte Ltd
33 Pekin Street #02-01
Far East Square
Singapore 048763

Library of Congress Control Number 2009929035

British Library Cataloguing in Publication data

A catalogue record for this book is available from the British Library

ISBN 978-1-84787-527-3
ISBN 978-1-84787-528-0 (pbk)

Typeset by C&M Digitals (P) Ltd, Chennai, India
Printed in Great Britain by TJ International Ltd, Padstow, Cornwall
Printed on paper from sustainable resources

Mixed Sources
Product group from well-managed
forests and other controlled sources
www.fsc.org Cert no. SGS-COC-2482
© 1996 Forest Stewardship Council
FSC

Dedication

To my granddaughter Isabelle and all of her generation

Contents

List of abbreviations

BAPS	British Association of Paediatric Surgeons
BEEL	Baby Effective Early Learning
C&LP	Community and Learning Partnership Co-ordinator
CAB	Citizens' Advice Bureau
CAF	Common Assessment Framework
CAIPE	Centre for the Advancement of Interprofessional Education
CAMHS	Child and Adolescent Mental Health Services
CC	Children's Centre
CPAG	Child Poverty Action Group
CPM	Childcare Partnership Manager
CWDC	Children's Workforce Development Council
DCSF	Department for Children, Schools and Families
DfEE	Department for Education and Employment
DfES	Department for Education and Science
DHSS	Department of Health and Social Security
DoH	Department of Health
EAZ	Education Action Zone
ECEC	Early Childhood Education and Care
ECM	Every Child Matters
EEC	Early Education Centre
EEC	Early Excellence Centre
EECERA	European Early Childhood Education Research Association
EPPE	Effective Provision of Pre-School Education
ESOL	English for Speakers of Other Languages
EYDCP	Early Years Development and Child Care Partnership
EYFS	Early Years Foundation Stage
EYP	Early Years Professional
EYPS	Early Years Professional Status
EYQIP	Early Years Quality Improvement Programme
FE	Further Education

GLF	Graduate Leader Fund
GP	General Practitioner (Medical Doctor)
GSCC	General Social Care Council
GTC	General Teaching Council
HAZ	Health Action Zone
ICC	Integrated Children's Centre
JAR	Joint Area Review
KEEP	Key Elements of Effective Practice
LA	Local Authority
MBA	Masters in Business Administration
MCS	Millenium Cohort Study
NCSL	National College for School Leadership
NESS	National Evaluation of Sure Start
NMC	Nursing and Midwifery Council
NPQH	National Professional Qualification for Headteachers
NPQICL	National Professional Qualification in Integrated Centre Leadership
OECD	Organisation for Economic Cooperation and Development
Ofsted	Office for Standards in Education, Children's Services and Skills
PATA	Parents and Teachers Association
PCT	Primary Care Trust
PSLA	Pre-School Learning Alliance
QCA	Qualifications and Curriculum Authority
QTS	Qualified Teacher Status
SENCO	Special Educational Needs Coordinator
SfC&D	Skills for Care and Development
SLAs	Service Level Agreements (between children's centres and outside providers of services such as day care)
SMT	Senior Management Team
SSLP	Sure Start Local Programme
TUPE	Transfer of Undertakings (Protection of Employment) Regulations
UNICEF	United Nations Children's Fund
WO	Welsh Office

Key for icons

Chapter objectives

Case study

Useful websites

Summary

Further reading

Points for reflection

Activity

Acknowledgements

The research which provided much of the first-hand data was carried out in spring 2008. One hundred and ninety questionnaires were sent out to heads and senior staff of children's centres with a letter explaining the purpose and 23 completed responses were received. The questions covered basic contextual information about their settings, their professional heritage and length of time in post. Questions explored their understanding of partnership working, the range of partners and the degree of partnership including awareness among partners of points of view other than their own, the most and least rewarding aspects of partnership working including factors that enabled or prevented success in their experience, and what raises or reduces their confidence. All were asked to provide condensed case studies to illustrate aspects of partnership working from practice and for examples of the use of language that enabled or confused. In selecting the examples quoted I have tried to reflect the balance of the tone of the responses received.

This book would not have been possible without a great deal of help from family and colleagues. In particular I wish to thank: colleagues in children's centres who responded to the questionnaire and others who have provided specific examples and photographs, including: Cynthia Knight and colleagues at St Thomas Centre, Birmingham; Elaine Stevens at Hately Heath Primary School and Children's Centre, Sandwell; Caroline Roberts at Ganney's Meadow Early Years Centre, Wirral; Elaine Johnston and colleagues at Fazakerley Children's Centre, Liverpool; Helen Cole and colleagues and parents from Cwmbran Integrated Children's Centre; colleagues in Local Authorities especially Birmingham, Brent, Camden, Medway, Nottinghamshire, Somerset and Staffordshire.

I also owe a great deal to colleagues I have worked with who have helped me to get to this point: to Chris Pascal and Tony Bertram who have been colleagues and supporters for many years and who encouraged me through difficult times; Paul Watling and Sue Webster for their encouragement and dialogue; Mary Briggs and Sue Barnett who kept me on the straight and narrow; Karen John and Sheila Thorpe for their friendship and support as my mentors; Anne McMullan for her encouragement; Maureen Saunders and Sarina Razzak for their quiet encouragement and in Sarina's case, invaluable advice with IT; Sean Delaney and Marjory Perkins for their cheerful enquiries.

Last but not least my heartfelt thanks go to my wife Janet and the family for their patience and practical help, and to Isabelle whose image kept me going when inspiration deserted me.

About the author

Michael Gasper is an Early Years consultant working as a trainer, coach, mentor and facilitator. He was a teacher for 27 years, 17 as a head, in a range of schools with children aged 4 to 13 before moving into Early Years and multi-agency research. He joined the Centre for Research in Early Childhood (CREC) in 1998, coordinating the team led by Professor Chris Pascal and Professor Tony Bertram on the Evaluation of the Early Excellence Centre programme for the DfES between 1999 and 2004. With Paul Watling he is co-convener for the mentor special interest group for the European Early Childhood Research Association (EECERA).

His interest in multi-agency working developed from his time as a head working with colleagues in Health and Social Services and subsequently, while engaged with Early Excellence, he worked with Sheila Thorpe to research the need for mentor support for leaders of multi-agency settings. He is a tutor, mentor and assessor on the National Professional Qualification in Integrated Centre Leadership (NPQICL) programme and has been involved since the pilot stage for a number of providers.

Michael has a passionate belief in the value of multi-agency settings in their own right, as well as their significance as a key component in the developing extended schools and community education programmes. His work with settings and leaders includes mentoring, training and research.

Introduction

When I began researching for this book I was struck by how few publications focused on this approach – multi-agency working. Significantly the majority of those that do are written from particular points of view in relation to their own profession, such as Weinstein, Whittington and Leiba whose focus is on social work and the research documented by Barr, Koppel, Reeves, Hammick and Freeth which investigates multi-agency working in the context of health. An important exception is the work of Angela Anning and her team who specifically researched multi-professional practice. There are references to multi-agency working in other publications and significantly more in more recent years. However, when you investigate multi-agency working *in the Early Years* there remains very little material, despite the emphasis on 'joined-up thinking' that has increased in the last ten years.

In exploring the issues around multi-agency practice in the Early Years several aspects will hopefully become clearer:

- There are features of multi-agency working which are universal.

- There are features of multi-agency working that are context-specific.

- To be successful requires visionary leadership.

- There are contradictions arising from different expectations.

- You have to be realistic about where you and your partners are starting from.

- The potential gains are exciting and do make a real difference to all involved.

- The consequences of not doing so can be disastrous.

The universal features are to do with the nature of relationships between people. All the writers acknowledge that the aims make sense: it is common sense to share information, to work in partnership and harmony, to recognise each others' potential contributions especially when trying to meet the needs of essentially the same people. They also acknowledge that, as Friedman suggests, we have to be realistic about our historical practices and predispositions to fully understand our starting points and to be in a good position to plan changes to 'turn the curve' and move towards new goals (Friedman, 2005). The ability to be open to the perspectives of other colleagues, to be willing to engage in dialogue to explore similarities and differences, to respect others and genuinely listen as well as speak, are essential whatever the context of developing multi-agency working.

The aspects that are context-specific are influenced by past and existing relationships between settings, families and communities and other professionals and agencies. They are to do with factors specific to the setting such as:

- the phase, size and location of the setting;

- staff numbers, skills, qualifications and range of professional backgrounds;

- the stage of team development;

- the relationship between the different elements of the reach area;

- the leadership style and approach of the setting head/manager;

- the relationships with those who provide or contribute to core services;

- the structure, attitude and expectation of local authority departments and officers.

In some cases settings demonstrate positive approaches and a sense of direction and generate new ideas and approaches while others struggle. You cannot ignore the context or pretend the constraints or opportunities are different from the reality presented. In order to be realistic the quality and experience of setting and local leadership is a critical factor, for the ethos and tone is often established by the leadership and can liberate or constrain (Dahlberg et al., 1999; Hargreaves and Fink, 2008).

The quality of leadership has been shown to be a critical ingredient for successful partnership working. Successful multi-agency leaders tend to show a capacity to be visionary and to see the positive potential in situations and people. They are able to stand back from the immediate, to reflect and to draw on different leadership styles and approaches to address issues. They welcome challenge and recognise change as inevitable. They listen and allow others to contribute, actively encouraging dialogue and discussion and being willing to seek new perspectives and follow alternative approaches. They are careful to nurture the potential in their team and to grow new leaders. They genuinely value and respect all they work with and tend to be open and non-judgemental. They are often financially aware, or can draw on someone who is, and are able to manage the difficult balance between freedom and form. Where the leadership style is limited or one-dimensional, where the approach is more rigid and less flexible, where it lacks tolerance of others and is reluctant to see or accept other perspectives, the success of partnership working is also limited, constrained and unlikely to be sustained.

Partnership working itself is complex and multi-dimensional. It is ground-breaking and is often seen as a challenge to established relationships, systems of organisation, hierarchies and power relationships. It requires innovative approaches in order to begin to work. It often involves bringing together people with differing views, all of whom believe their view and 'way' is right, and professions with differing approaches to practice, all of which believe their approach is 'proper' or the only way. In this potential maelstrom it is easy to lose sight of the child, the family and community in the struggle to maintain power, influence, control and dominance.

Multi-agency settings such as children's centres are using innovative approaches to leadership where roles and responsibilities are clear but hierarchies are flattened. The leaders themselves model approaches that they wish staff to adopt when working with children, parents and colleagues and they model these approaches when meeting with colleagues from other agencies and professions. Non-judgemental and open approaches where dialogue, reflection and discussion help shape policy and practice and where contributions from all are encouraged and everyone is valued have been shown to work well in establishing positive relationships with partners and within teams. However, these same approaches are immensely challenging to those for whom a 'top down' model is the only way of working. They can and do generate tension where partners are used to structured and hierarchical approaches where those at lower tiers do as they are told by their line managers. Leaders have to be able to deal with contradictions and their practical implications.

Some of the contradictions are to do with differing government agendas and priorities. For example, the national targets to address health, employment and poverty issues generate top-down pressures, but the system advocated and encouraged for partnership working is essentially bottom-up. Targets to encourage healthy diet and reductions in obesity, smoking and alcohol abuse can create anxiety and undermine attempts to improve confidence and well-being, particularly if there is a lack of consultation between the partners involved. The emphasis on improving attachment and supporting the quality of family life for babies and parents in the first year does not sit well with the government's drive to have more women in work; accessible childcare can mean parents use a large number of different carers in any week which undermines the child's well-being and confidence.

The aims of children's centres represent a different approach. They set out to work with children, parents, families and communities to identify needs and then to meet them. This approach requires different relationships from the traditional well established models where an external expert is trusted to know and to advise or recommend. Their approach to policy and to finance does not follow traditional pathways because the way services are provided and funded, and the staff who run them, is often innovative and has no existing form or model. This can be a challenge accepted positively with new forms worked out in practice, but can also be approached in a negative way which imposes an existing and inappropriate system. The same is true of the timescales involved in identifying, planning and providing services, and the way their success is monitored and measured.

Multi-agency also means multi-dimensional. Those engaged in multi-agency working have to be realistic and understand they are dealing with complexity, even if they cannot see how to begin to disentangle the jumble of strands of interests and opinions. In this respect starting with the children and parents or carers can provide a clearer focus, especially for those closest to them. For leaders of multi-agency work the task is harder, mainly because of the complex relationships, perceptions of power and authority, influences of specific professional training and practice, constraints of regulations whether real or perceived, and pressures of time and finance. All those involved have to be realistic about where they are starting from and what has to be put in place to support how they want to move forward.

The benefits of partnership working have been shown to work at different levels. The use of a single key worker located in a particular site has helped individuals and families to improve their levels of confidence and well-being and to become self-sufficient. The level of trust between members of partnership teams and the families and communities has enabled a real and equal partnership where needs can be identified and met. Partnerships between professionals and agencies have meant better access to services and an avoidance of duplication and greater consistency in approaches which in turn has meant services have been delivered in a more efficient and cost-effective way. The potential positive effects on children and their longer-term ability to thrive, learn and contribute have been noted by research such as the Effective Provision of Pre-School Education (EPPE – see DfES, 1997–2004) study and partnership working can contribute significantly to this. The need for supporting mothers and babies to establish secure relationships and bonding which underpin their well-being and confidence are also important areas of partnership work through children's centre teams.

Where there is an absence of partnership working or where it breaks down, the consequences can be unthinkable. The examples of Victoria Climbié and Baby 'P' must serve as a spur to all to work towards improved partnerships and better quality provision.

Who is this book for?

This book is primarily for practitioners and undergraduates but will be of interest to anyone who has to work in a multi-agency context or is interested in knowing more. Multi-agency working is referred to as partnership working throughout as a generic term.

What does it cover?

- Chapter 1 sets the scene and examines what partnership working is, why it is important and how it has developed.

- Chapter 2 explores what partnership working looks like and the associated benefits.

- Chapter 3 uses three case studies from other countries which have influenced partnership working development and looks more closely at the way political emphasis has influenced developments in partnership working in England and Wales.

- Chapter 4 uses examples to illustrate how partnership working is put into practice.

- Chapter 5 focuses more closely on identifying needs and benefits to children, parents and communities.

- Chapter 6 looks at the challenges that face leaders in meeting the changes required to support successful partnership working. This chapter also looks at key differences between schools and children's centres.

- Chapter 7 looks at the new professionals and the current and future skills and training they will need.

The book provides a short summary at the start of each chapter and key points are set out at the end. Reflection points and action points are inserted into the text to encourage the reader to consider aspects of the issues raised and their implications for practice. Hopefully the reader will engage with these points and get the most out of them.

The many examples provided by colleagues are real cases but the anonymity of settings and individuals is respected and names have been changed to maintain confidentiality. Where cases are constructions to illustrate specific kinds of actions or responses, this is clearly indicated.

1

What is partnership working, where did it come from and why is it important?

> This chapter introduces the term 'partnership working', where it has come from, why it holds an important place within government agendas for change and what it means within the context of Early Childhood Education and Care (ECEC) organisation and practice. The chapter explores definitions of associated terms to clarify different ways in which partnerships can be conceived and constructed and what these mean in practical terms to practitioners, families, children and communities.
>
> Chapter themes are:
>
> - What is partnership working?
> - Where did partnership working come from?
> - What are the associated terms, their definitions, similarities and differences?
> - Why is partnership working important?
> - How has the move towards greater partnership working developed?
> - What is partnership working in practice: benefits, challenges and leadership?

So what do we mean by partnership working (multi-agency working) and what is it all about? Why is it important? Where did it come from and how did it develop into a national policy?

What is partnership working in this context?

Partnership working is a key concept at the core of social and educational policy since the start of the millennium. It is evidence of a shift in emphasis at government, local and setting levels away from a 'top-down' approach towards a 'bottom-up' approach. This shift came from a fundamental change in philosophy which included recognition of the importance of working with service users more closely to help identify needs and how they could be met. This was very different from the previous approach which tended to dictate what would be provided for service users and was based on a view of service organisation and delivery that was separated into and focused on specialism. The previous philosophy took more account of what those in specialist services such as Education, Health and Social Services believed was right for people, rather than listening to what people themselves might say they needed. The more recent definition, organisation and provision of services for children, parents, families and communities by government and local authorities still recognises the need for specialism within service providers but also places a new emphasis on 'joined-up thinking' and working. This change grounded in social theories recognises the value of the principle of including all perspectives, including those who need and use the services, so that what is provided is more relevant and appropriate in matching needs, more efficient in delivery and achieves more effective outcomes. An example of joined-up working in practice is Camden in London and the way they have built their multi-agency team supporting Early Years. The team developed from their original Sure Start Local Programmes (see Useful websites at the end of the chapter). Specialists from a wide range of services including speech and language, midwives, specialist support for the Somali community, librarians and child protection were paid for by the local authority to work as multi-agency support for four days each week and to return to specialist work for the remaining day. The arrangements have been developed to reach and serve a wider community than the original Sure Start areas and professionals have been nurtured who are skilled in planned multi-agency approaches to service provision. The reduction in funding has led to a review to assess how best to continue developing the teams to meet future needs.

Partnership working provides opportunities for needs to be met collectively as well as individually so that the needs of whole families can be addressed in a unified way. Partnership working is embodied in the notion of children, parents, families and communities having access to a wide range of support and developmental services to enable them to:

- identify what their needs are;

- access the most appropriate help from all relevant agencies;

- begin to take greater control of their own lives;

- increase their confidence and self-worth;

- develop their skills and extend their education;

- enable them to live more fulfilled lives and contribute more fully to wider society.

Partnership working is also about professional agencies aiming to improve the way they organise, plan, undertake and reflect on their work jointly as elements of a team, each with their own perspectives and skills but combining effectively as a unified whole. Whereas previously individuals had to attend a range of locations often at some distance, a key principle of partnership working is to reduce this to local sites, initially targeted at areas of high deprivation and then extended, so that children, parents and families can receive the support they need wherever they live. Clearly specialist centres remain – there will always need to be surgeries, hospitals, schools and care centres – but the emphasis is for services to be brought to neighbourhood locations wherever possible. Phrases such as 'joined-up thinking' and 'one-stop shop' capture the emphasis of partnership working.

 Case study

Partnerships developing over time – combining Health, Social Care and Early Years

Ganney's Meadow is a children's centre in an area of high deprivation in the Wirral, housed in part of a refurbished junior school building. In the early 1990s, due to falling rolls, all the primary aged children were accommodated in the adjoining infant building; the local nursery school was relocated into one wing of the empty junior building in line with the local authority's aim of developing their first integrated centre. At this time social care staff rented a couple of rooms and ran a family support group – drop-ins and adult courses which were very low key – in the vacant wing of the building with a locked door between them and the nursery school. These were the first staff that actually integrated with the 'nursery school staff'.

The specialist practitioner nurse role was part of this development of integrated services. One of the governors (a health visitor herself) helped the setting to develop this idea and which led to liaison with the Primary Care Trust (PCT) who agreed to fund the post if the centre allocated a room. The health practitioner on site was and still is funded through the PCT. The salary has never come out of centre budgets.

The refurbishment of the additional space/wing was funded through Early Excellence Centre (EEC) (see Glossary) finance in the late 1990s in order to provide a crèche, training rooms, a family room and a multi-purpose room for a range of groups for 0–3s with their parents. The funding to relocate the local branch library came from the local authority's chief executive and the 0–3s day care came later, funded through the Neighbourhood Nursery initiative.

This example shows how partnership working has developed over time and how different initiatives have been used to develop and extend the organisation, staffing and range of services.

Where did partnership working come from?

To some extent there has always been recognition of the value and importance of joint working and shared information, particularly within organisations. Within Health, Social Services and Education different specialist branches have used joint meetings to evaluate needs and plan actions. Cooperation between pairs of agencies, such as Education and Health or Health and Social Services, have also been well established. For example, hospitals included a welfare department to assist patients and to liaise with Social Services and other agencies. Social Services have been responsible for calling and chairing joint meetings to address child protection issues. Child protection case conferences are focused on the needs of the child. They have brought together representatives from Education, Health, the police, drug and alcohol counsellors and other agencies relevant to specific cases. Within Education the school doctor and school nurse focused on the needs of children with medical needs, alerting the school to specific needs of individuals and linking with Social Services where issues beyond medical needs were involved. Key features of these kinds of cooperation are that they were controlled by the professional agencies, they tended to be in response to a crisis and while they were intended to be supportive and did attempt to allow a voice to the individuals 'at risk', in practice it was often very difficult for the individual or family to make an effective contribution. The increasing emphasis on inter-agency cooperation is illustrated in two successive papers: *Working Together: A Guide to Arrangements for Inter-agency Co-operation for the Protection of Children from Abuse* (DHSS, 1986) and *Working Together to Safeguard and Promote the Welfare of Children: A Guide to Inter-agency Working to Safeguard and Promote the Welfare of Children* (DoH, Home Office and DfEE, 1999). The gradual combining of Health and Social Services and the creation of new government units, such as the Children's and Young People's Unit in 2000, was supported by a series of government papers following the turn of the century. The emphasis changed from departments which dictated to departments and units that encouraged professionals to facilitate and empower families to take responsibility for themselves (Pascall, 1986: 38). The shift in emphasis was also influenced by the growth in understanding nationally and internationally of the interdependence of Health, Social Welfare and Education, supported by research such as the OECD reports *Starting Strong I* and *II* (2001 and 2006).

While this kind of cooperation has continued, what has changed is the 'top-down' emphasis. There has been a growing emphasis on equality and real partnership to allow the true 'voice' of individuals and families to be heard, combined with a clear aim of identifying and addressing need, preferably before reaching crisis dimensions. During the 1990s Social Services established family centres in areas identified as having high social deprivation. These centres were run by a leader from Social Services but aimed to include parents and families in the planning and running of services. This model was later developed and extended in both Sure Start and Early Excellence Centres but is mentioned here to illustrate the shift in thinking and emphasis.

Defining terms

Defining terms in a way that will be clearly understood by all is a challenging task. Each of the key agencies involved in early years care and education partnerships – Community Work, Education, Social Services, Health, Housing, Family Support, counselling services for drug and alcohol abuse – has their own professional language and code, including acronyms, and often employ the same words with completely different meanings. For example, the term for agencies working together is presented in different ways:

- inter-agency

- multi-agency

- inter-disciplinary

- inter-professional

- multi-professional

- multi-disciplinary.

These describe different kinds of combinations, the first two organisationally based practice and the latter three types of organisation (Weinstein et al., 2003). These can be intentional or accidental, formal or informal, structured or loose. The current preferred term is partnership working but even this may not capture appropriately the subtle ethos or underlying desire for new ways of developing and refining the complex warp and weft of professional relationships focused on improvement for families and children. Nevertheless this is the term that will be used throughout the book.

Whittington (in Weinstein et al., 2003) provides the following definitions of partnership and collaboration:

> Partnership is a state of relationship, at organizational, group, professional or inter-professional level, to be achieved, maintained and reviewed.
>
> Collaboration is an active process of partnership in action.

Two other definitions are given by the UK Centre for the Advancement of Interprofessional Education (CAIPE) and quoted by Barr et al. (2005), the first of which emphasises the combination of adult learning principles with collaborative learning and practice, but within the context of a rationale which takes account of all possible combinations including inter-personal, inter-group, organisational and inter-organisational relationships and processes. The second simplifies this to a situation where any two or more professionals share learning 'with, from and about each other' to develop and improve collaborative practice. In other words, the definitions stress the active sharing of professional practice at individual, group and organisational levels in order to improve understanding and collaboration, which Barr et al. refer to as 'interprofessional education', as opposed to 'multiprofessional education' which involves any occasion when people from two or more professions learn side by side but not necessarily with the intention of improving collaboration and the quality of their work.

There does need to be a distinction between the different levels of collaboration and interaction: professionals may be housed together or co-located, which may or may not involve sharing information; they may be working jointly where there is a degree of information sharing; they may be more unified in their approach and working systematically with higher degrees of information sharing, planning and review; or there may be a merging into a single organised unit to achieve agreed common aims. Within a specifically Early Years context this view is supported by Anning et al. (2006) who suggest a hierarchy of terms to describe different levels of partnership which echo this progression (Anning et al., 2006: 6).

Weinstein et al. define the need for successful *inter-professional* collaboration as:

> ... practitioners learning:

- what is common to the professional involved
- the *distinctive contribution* of each profession

- what may be *complementary* between them
- what may be in tension or conflict between them

and

- how to work together ...

(2003: 49)

The distinction between learning side by side and learning *about each other* is critical to the underlying theme of this book, which is to improve shared understanding and assist practitioners and researchers alike in raising their awareness of the complexities involved in partnership working.

 Points for reflection

Does this match your experience?

How would you define agencies working together?

What other definitions can you find or suggest?

If defining terms is complex, identifying and finding a common pathway through definitions of practice values, codes of practice and ethics is even more so. Each profession has their own outlook and values and their own priorities. Within a profession different skill areas have their own points of view and stress different aspects, and each has their own way of looking at situations, interpreting them and identifying critical aspects to address. It remains important for each profession and agency to have clear aims and to retain their identity and the ability to make decisions and take actions independently. In addition, however, they must also develop a greater understanding of other professional points of view and cultures and actively improve cooperation and coordination and work towards greater integration. Within complex organisations such as Health, there is a growing understanding of the value and practice of more coordinated and combined approaches (Barr et al., 2005) and greater understanding of how this can be achieved (Freeth et al., 2005).

Why is it important?

During the 1990s a series of research reports pointed to the effects of poverty:

> Children from poorer homes have a lower life expectancy, are more likely to die in infancy or childhood, have a greater likelihood of infections and poor health, a lower chance of educational attainment, a higher probability of involvement in crime and homelessness, and a higher risk of teenage pregnancy.
>
> (Holterman, 1994)

Kelly (2008) also shows the critical importance of housing to child health. This seems to suggest that families in poverty are likely to be involved with a wide range of agencies, for largely negative reasons. It seems entirely logical and necessary, therefore, for agencies to work together to address the effects of poverty in the first instance if they are to break the spiral of deprivation which repeats through generations and as a first step towards reducing poverty itself. Since the late 1990s there has been an increasing emphasis from the government for greater sharing of information and cooperation within and between agencies. The Utting Report *People Like Us – the Report of the Review of Safeguards for Children Living Away from Home* (DoH/WO, 1997) drew attention to the inadequacies of provision for children taken into care. In her summary to the House of Lords Baroness Jay referred to:

> The report presents a woeful tale of failure at all levels to provide a secure and decent childhood for some of the most vulnerable children … The report reveals that in far too many cases not enough care was taken. Elementary safeguards were not in place or not enforced. Many children were harmed rather than helped. The review reveals that these failings were not just the fault of individuals – though individuals were at fault. It reveals the failures of a whole system. (Baroness Jay of Paddington, statement to the House of Lords, 19 November 1997, Hansard)

This report reinforced the findings emerging throughout the 1990s regarding the consequences of child poverty and served to bring new policies into place to raise standards of health, social care and education for children including those cared for by local authorities, and successive initiatives such as Early Excellence Centre (EEC) Evaluation (2002), the Effective Provision of Pre-School Education (EPPE – DfES, 2004) and the National Evaluation of Sure Start (NESS – 2005 and 2007) have provided evidence of real benefits to children, families and communities where more joined-up working takes place.

In recent times the consequences of agencies not working together have been starkly bleak. There has been powerful evidence from specific cases that we cannot afford to see Early Childhood Education and Care (ECEC) in isolation and need to move towards greater cooperation and coordination of services, especially for vulnerable children and families. The failure of agencies to communicate internally and with each other has contributed directly to dire consequences, illustrated by the tragic case of Victoria Climbié which led to fundamental changes in approach and lent a new urgency to the need for effective inter-agency working. The consequent report (Laming Report, 2003), led to more formal procedures and a government White Paper, *Every Child Matters: Change for Children* (DfES, 2004). The recommendations of this report are still in the process of being implemented and underpin revisions of childcare policy and practice, for example through the Common Assessment Framework (CAF) which has been set in place in an attempt to improve partnership working where children and families 'at risk' are identified. However, the case of 'Baby P' and events in Haringey which came to light in 2008 and Darlington in 2009 serve as a reminder that there is still a long way to go before there can be greater confidence in the systems in place. Perhaps the real need is for constant vigilance.

> The Common Assessment Framework (CAF) is a key part of delivering frontline services that are integrated and focused around the needs of children and young people. The CAF is a standardized approach to conducting an assessment of a child's additional needs and deciding how those needs should be met.
> (www.everychildmatters. gov.uk/deliveringservices/caf/)

More recently, in a joint statement in 2007, the professional bodies representing Social Care, Nursing and Education (the General Social Care Council (GSCC), the

Nursing and Midwifery Council (NMC) and the General Teaching Council (GTC)) acknowledged shared values and included recognition of the need to work together:

> Children's practitioners value the contribution that a range of colleagues make to children and young people's lives, and they form effective relationships across the children's workforce. Their integrated practice is based on a willingness to bring their own expertise to bear on the pursuit of shared goals, and a respect for the expertise of others.
> (www.nmc-uk.org.uk/aArticle.aspx?ArticleID=2344)

The main benefits from partnership working for children, families and communities can be summarised as follows:

- It is more efficient:

  - There is a better chance for individuals to be heard.
  - Needs are more likely to be identified.
  - Needs can be dealt with holisitically and with regard to the whole family where necessary.
  - Resources are more focused and there is less risk of duplication.
  - Agencies' actions complement each other.

- It is more effective:

  - Individuals are valued and listened to and their confidence and self-esteem is enhanced.
  - The support is focused on empowerment not dependency.
  - Networking between agencies about individuals can reduce bureaucracy and save time.
  - Actions are part of a more coherent shared strategy.

The National Evaluation of Sure Start Summary Report of 2007 noted the following key strategic points:

What worked at strategic level was:

- systemic, sustainable structures in governance and management/leadership;
- a welcoming, informal but professional ethos;
- empowering parents, children and practitioners.

What worked at operational level was:

- auditing and responding to community priorities in universal services;
- early identification and targeting of children and parents to benefit from specialist services;
- recruiting, training and deploying providers with appropriate qualifications and personal attributes; and
- managing the complexities of multi-agency teamwork.

(Anning et al., 2007)

This report did raise additional issues which need to be addressed, particularly in terms of ensuring services reach those in most need and drawing attention to the need for flexibility in organisation, times and availability of services and specific agencies. What it affirms are the underlying advantages and gains from partnership working in identifying and addressing the needs of children, families and communities ...

Activity

What were the key findings of the Laming Report?

Can you find evidence that the findings and recommendations are being acted upon?

How has the move towards greater partnership working developed?

The short answer is that there was a growing understanding that the service structures and relationships were no longer adequate to meet changing needs, and that this combined with a growing understanding of the consequences of poverty in terms of health, social and educational deprivation. This realisation prompted consultation by government on a much wider basis than previously which helped uncover evidence from examples provided by families themselves and grassroots practitioners of all professional heritages as well as from research findings. Effective lobbying from early years, health and social care professionals and academics reinforced political emphasis on holistic approaches to break cycles of deprivation by developing shared understanding and a more coherent and joined-up practice. Changing theory into practice proved to be complex but has been undertaken in a considered and structured process which has drawn on views from all stakeholders. Baldock et al. (2005: 15–34) and Clark and Waller (2007: 28–33) provide comprehensive histories charting political changes. Figure 1.1 shows some of the more significant changes since 1980.

Many of the new initiatives acknowledged the need for and encouraged the closer cooperation and direct involvement of parents. An example of this is provided by the Early Years Development and Child Care Partnerships (see Figure 1.2).

In 1997 the new government insisted that local authorities establish Early Years Development and Childcare Partnerships (EYDCPs). These groups brought together all those involved in pre-school and early years care and education from the private, voluntary and state sectors (see Figure 1.3 for an example). All had to be represented and their initial aim was to share information, audit what was already in place and identify needs. This then extended to shared organisation, planning and delivery of services to children, including sharing training and development to improve the overall quality of service. The local authority role was meant to facilitate and not to lead within the partnership. Funding for initiatives such as training was made available from government, subject to the acceptance of a successful bid based on a specific plan.

The EYDCPs kick-started a form of partnership working which benefitted the private and independent sector in particular and meant that when stricter registration and inspection was introduced, standards had already been enhanced and there was a supportive body already in place to offer help if needed.

1980	***Enabling legislation***
As a new head teacher partnership is with school governors and Education, Health and Social Service separately.	
Schools are separated from local authorities.	
Increased government emphasis on freedom of choice means parents are encouraged to choose and to take an active part in partnership with schools.	1989 *Managing Service More Effectively – Performance Review* (Audit Commission)
The profile and voice of Early Years gradually increases.Vouchers are introduced to enable greater access to pre-school education.	1989 The Children Act
	National Standards for under 8s day care and childminders
1990	
Greater cooperaton developed between Health and Education particularly for children with additional needs.	
Closer cooperative working between agencies exists but depends on informal structures.	
1997	
New Labour – impetus to include all partners in Early Years Development and Childcare Partnerships (EYDCPs).	1998 *Supporting Families: A Consultation Document* (DoH)
Single Regeneration Budget.	2001 *Working Together Under the Children Act* (DoH)
Working family tax credit changes encourage pre-school childcare.	2002 *Integrated Services for Older People: Building a Whole System Approach in England* (Audit Commission) – 'whole systems' approach
Education Action Zones, Health Action Zones.	
2004	
Early Excellence Centres, Sure Start, Neighbourhood Nurseries — make pre-school more widely available, increase quality and encourage agencies to work more closely together.	2004 *Every Child Matters: Change for Children*
	2004 *The Children Act*
Children's Centres.	2006 *The Childcare Act*
Parents are seen as equal partners.	Pre-school education and care no longer separate
Multi-agency working in practice.	EYPS introduced
2008	2007 *The Children's Plan* – EYFS
A Children's Centre available to all by 2010.	

Figure 1.1   The changing face of partnership working

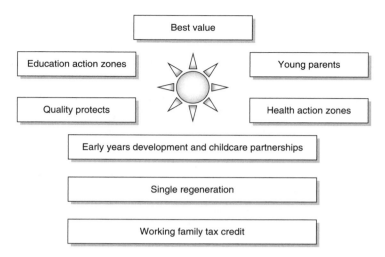

Figure 1.2 Initiatives increasing the emphasis on parental involvement

---

Nottinghamshire Early Years Development and Childcare Partnership (EYDCP)

We are the Nottinghamshire Early Years Development and Childcare Partnership (EYDCP). We were set up in 1998. We bring together local partners to:

- develop and deliver free early years education for three- and four-year-olds
- develop childcare services for children under 16
- help to deliver Sure Start services.

Our members include childcare providers, maintained and independent schools, local employers, health services, voluntary organisations, Ofsted, Nottinghamshire County Council, Learning and Skills Council and Jobcentre Plus.
Nottinghamshire County Council is responsible for providing leadership, planning services, co-ordinating the way services are delivered and consulting children, parents and carers. It is also responsible for managing our finances and must monitor our performance.

www.nottinghamshire.gov.uk/home/learningandwork/preschool/earlyyearseducation/eydcp.htm

---

Figure 1.3 An EYDCP example from Nottinghamshire
Reproduced with permission from Nottinghamshire Children's and Young People's Service

In addition three key programmes came into being: Early Excellence Centres (EECs), Sure Start and Neighbourhood Nurseries (see Figure 1.4). Many current children's centres retain their original parent title in their name.

Activity

Find out what were the key similarities and differences between these initiatives.

What is their legacy today?

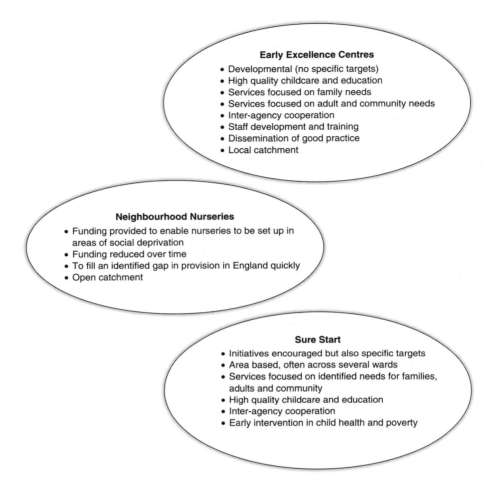

Early Excellence Centres
- Developmental (no specific targets)
- High quality childcare and education
- Services focused on family needs
- Services focused on adult and community needs
- Inter-agency cooperation
- Staff development and training
- Dissemination of good practice
- Local catchment

Neighbourhood Nurseries
- Funding provided to enable nurseries to be set up in areas of social deprivation
- Funding reduced over time
- To fill an identified gap in provision in England quickly
- Open catchment

Sure Start
- Initiatives encouraged but also specific targets
- Area based, often across several wards
- Services focused on identified needs for families, adults and community
- High quality childcare and education
- Inter-agency cooperation
- Early intervention in child health and poverty

Figure 1.4   Key features of Early Excellence Centres, Neighbourhood Nurseries and Sure Start

During the first five years of the New Labour administration, research into these initiatives grew and increased overall awareness and understanding of the need to see professional support more holistically, with Social Services, Health and Education addressing the needs of families collectively. Local authorities in many areas combined Education and Social Services departments under titles more focused on family needs and Community Development grew in importance. Partnerships with private and voluntary sector organisations became increasingly common. There was an expectation that professionals would improve joined-up thinking by consulting more fully, sharing information, working in harmony to identify needs and defining strategies to meet them together. The initiatives called for new models of organisation and communication at setting, local authority and regional levels.

In Wales, Scotland and Northern Ireland Sure Start and Early Years initiatives have been organised differently. The new edition of Baldock et al. (2009) provides a good overview.

There was a clear expectation that service users and the wider local community would be included more equally in identifying their needs and appropriate services to meet them. Critically, funding for these initiatives was available for local authorities through a bidding process.

Change was enabled by the Children Act 2004 which focused on five areas:

- Be healthy

- Stay safe

- Enjoy and achieve

- Make a positive contribution

- Achieve economic well-being.

It emphasised:

- greater public recognition of children's rights;

- greater consultation;

- agencies working more closely together.

It was complemented by the Childcare Act 2006 which placed the lead responsibility for creating and maintaining local care networks on local authorities. There was a new emphasis on ascertaining local needs and of working with and for the community, families, carers and children. In an interview for the BBC in 2006, Gordon Brown referred to the role of government being that of 'servant to the community', encapsulating the shift in relationships.

Research has shown that these experiments in partnership working have had considerable success for children, families and local communities (DfES, 1997–2004; Bertram and Pascal, 2000; Bertram et al., 2002; NESS, 2008; Quinton, 2004). As time has gone on the emphasis has changed. The three initiatives highlighted have been drawn together to form children's centres and there has been a new expectation that services should become 'sustainable' as funding has been reduced. The emergence of Every Child Matters has added a new emphasis and imperative with clear timescales for implementation. Initiatives such as Extended Schools have gained impetus. This is not to suggest a smooth pathway with all loose ends joined up. Not all is plain sailing and not all is for the best. Some of the issues will be explored in the following chapters.

Alongside the national changes, European and worldwide understanding has also shifted and led to statements of principle such as the UN Convention on the Rights of the Child, ratified by the UK in 1991. There was already a European convention dating from 1950, the European Convention on Human Rights, which was a reaction to the Nazi era. In addition, technological advances have accelerated the ability of researchers to communicate and share research findings. This in turn has contributed to the increase in knowledge and understanding of ECEC and the influence of successful approaches such as those developed in Italy in Reggio Emilia and in New Zealand with *Te Whaariki,* which are explored in Chapter 3. The move towards more inclusive and holistic approaches and partnership working is not restricted to the UK.

 Points for reflection

What are the key benefits of agencies working together?

What challenges face those involved?

What needs to be done to help service users to take an active and equal part?

Partnership working in practice

While Chapters 3 and 4 deal with this in more depth, some indication of practical aspects may be helpful. Partnership working is a way of making the expertise and experience of a wide range of people each with different skills and perspectives available to each other as they come together and find new ways to address needs. The process of sharing involves open dialogue which is a dynamic and creative force: through listening, talking and exchanging ideas, new understanding develops. Dahlberg et al. (1999: 139) describe the difficulty of establishing a culture of critical dialogue and the danger that criticism will be taken personally, stressing the need to treat critical dialogue as 'a way to reconstruct our work'. This is particularly difficult with dialogue between agencies with different professional heritages and languages, especially when the same word can carry a very different meaning.

In addition there are clear gains in terms of more effective use of time and resources if issues are approached jointly rather than separately. The scenario in the case study below is entirely fictional but serves to illustrate some of the potential value of partnership working.

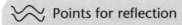 Case study

A family of five

Zac 3 months, Della 2 years 3 months, Wayne 5; mother, Jess 20, suffers with anxiety and depression; partner, Sasha 25, unemployed, is dependent on alcohol. Zac is the only child from the current relationship. Agencies involved currently with members of the family are: School, GP, Health Visitor, Social Services, Drug and Alcohol Counselling Service, Housing.

The family have recently moved into the area and there are no previous records available. They have been housed temporarily in a two-bedroom flat on the third floor of a three-storey block on a large estate with few amenities. Wayne has started school but the reception teacher has observed that he is solitary, listless and never appears to smile. There have been several occasions when Wayne has been late at the start of the day and no one has collected him until well after the end. The health visitor is concerned that Zac is not gaining weight.

If these agencies operate entirely separately or even in small cooperative groups, there is a strong possibility that advice and treatment will only address the immediate issues, not the underlying causes. Advice and help may even be contra-dictory: for example, the school may insist on better time-keeping, unaware that this will add pressure; the GP may prescribe anti-depressants and recommend rest, which may well have side effects including tiredness. All would be offered in good faith and meet the specific aims of each organisation but may not really identify or address the deeper needs of the family. Time constraints and poorly framed target setting tend to lead to short-term approaches. Short-termism tends to be focused on the middle: those at either end of the spectrum of needs tend miss out: they do not 'fit' the system. Partnership working offers a different approach starting from a different set of values. It is based on an approach that is holistic, child and family centred, with the professionals serving needs that children and families themselves have helped define and with solutions that match the children and families rather than the reverse.

If services operate in a more cohesive way and one agency can act as coordinator between them and work directly with the family, all the issues can be aired and the needs of each member of the family assessed and prioritised. In many cases it is children's centres that provide the link and professionals from Health and Social Services are usually part of the core staff team or operate from the same site.

The advantages of partnership working have been known for some time and have been confirmed by research and evaluation. In 2007 Bruce and Meggitt noted that partnership working provided flexibility in the type and timing of services, allowing a balanced mix of families by providing care and education for all, not just those in severe need. Allowing for flexibility has been a key aspect of partnership work-ing, particularly where this is focused on needs identified by families and commu-nities themselves. Where possible, timings are arranged to match need rather than being limited to 'traditional' timings, and this is echoed by the move towards extended school provision. This has the additional advantage of allowing parents to work where this is what they wish. Bruce and Meggitt also comment on the ben-efits in terms of increased quality of both care and education which are echoed by NESS, and which encourage holistic approaches to child development.

By 2002 the evaluation of government initiatives then in process confirmed the positive benefits. In their annual evaluation of the Early Excellence Centre initia-tive Bertram et al. (2002) referred to the benefits of partnership working as enabling individuals 'to have a voice that is heard by all agencies involved' as well as providing easy access to a wide range of agencies and services. In particular Bertram et al. (2002) point to the increased ability of partner agencies to identify needs and jointly plan action to help families move towards greater independence rather than the reverse, thus avoiding duplication and allowing more efficient targeting of resources and greater cost-effectiveness.

Further reinforcement of the benefits were confirmed by NESS (2005) and by 2007 these benefits had become embedded in government thinking and planning, underpinning the anticipated effects clearly stated in *The Children's Plan* (DCSF), 2007). There is a strong emphasis on placing the needs of children and families first and on consultation to ensure that services match the requirements identified by them, rather than by agencies or the state. This change represents a major shift in policy and provides clear expectations of all involved. There is a stated aim to locate services 'under one roof in the places people visit frequently' in order to make them

truly accessible. There is an explicit recognition of the need to 'invest in all those who work with children'. The report makes provision for increasing capacity for working across professional boundaries.

The benefits of partnership working are enhanced where integrated centres are established by developing trust through regular contact with parents from an early stage, thus providing opportunities for issues to be raised and discussed sooner. Instead of parents feeling isolated they have access to a key worker who will try to encourage them to recognise their needs and seek help. The professionals are accessible, not distant, approachable, not hidden behind a wall of red tape, and motivated to answer the child's and parents' needs. Chapter 3 sets out case studies which show more detail of the benefits of partnership working.

The context in which partnership working takes place is important and this book explores the way children's centres provide an ethos, organisational structure and physical location for partnership working. In many cases they also provide the leadership essential to successful partnership working.

Leaders of children's centres are currently recruited from a very wide range of professional backgrounds and experience. *The Children's Workforce Strategy* was a consultation paper (DfES, 2003a) which recognised the need to remodel and led to new qualifications becoming available through university programmes. A clearer picture of the skills required has now emerged and is embodied in the National Standards for Leaders of Sure Start Children's Centres. There is now a clear intention for Early Years leaders and others to achieve parity of professional pay and conditions with those in Education and this has been enhanced by the National Professional Qualification for Integrated Centre Leadership (NPQICL), which emerged in 2005 and has equal status with the headteacher's qualification, the National Professional Qualification for Headteachers (NPQH). The leadership is mainly female and there is a wide range of qualifications among those in post, including those whose experience provides sufficient qualification in its own right. However, all children's centre leaders now have to hold the NPQICL. An unpublished study involving 21 children's centre leaders carried out in the summer of 2008 matched some of the findings of Aubrey (2007: 69), revealing that the majority came from a background in education, including pre-school, statutory school, and higher and further education, followed by social work, with significantly fewer from health, including nursing, midwifery and health visiting, or from other management background experience. What this does suggest is that the range of leaders' previous experience is wide, which is also reflected in the evaluations for NPQICL conducted by Whalley et al. (2008). Given the way that children's centres have emerged from Sure Start and the short timescale, it will take some time for training and qualification to catch up. The training provides grounding and opportunities to explore theory linked directly to practice, and also linked with critical reflection and critical dialogue. The groups taking part in training are enhanced by the range of experience as are the settings, and this needs be guarded as a diverse and rich source of potential for innovation and change. There is the potential for children's centre leadership to be free from the constraints of 'established' systems and better able to meet the demands for flexible approaches to identifying and meeting the needs of children, families and communities (NESS, 2007). Many of the leaders have been attracted to their posts because of the challenge and the opportunity to be agents for change.

Partnership working is not easy. Two children's centre leaders made the following comments when interviewed for the research on which this book as based.

> There are huge differences outside of Sure Start and children's centres as to the meaning and way to develop inter-agency/partnership working and it isn't all positive. It cannot be developed from a top-down bureaucratic structure and needs real commitment from all engaged in the process and it constantly changes. Not everyone is suited to this way of working.

> I have found that it takes time, patience and mutual respect to begin to develop partnership working. I found that by making links with other service managers in the area – through 1–1 meetings to talk ideas through – often brings dividends. It is easier to talk through possible issues outside of a general meeting. Managers (including myself) prefer to know in advance what is being suggested. Good coffee always helps!!

This begins to show some of the features of partnership working which will be explored in later chapters.

Since the late 1990s the movement towards more joined-up working, encouraged by government-funded initiatives, has enabled practitioners and families to work creatively together to develop social, health, care, support and educational services which are more closely matched to need, more accessible and more cost-effective. There has been greater opportunity for research and theory funded by government for example the evalutions for the Early Excellence Center programme (Bertram and Pascal EEC Evaluation Reports 2000, 2001, 2002) and the longitudinal studies for Effective Provision of Pre-School Education (EPPE Sylva et al., 2004) and National Evaluation of Sure Start (NESS Sylva et al., 2000 to date) to provide new ways of combining professional support and care and greater attention has been paid to recommendations. Theory has become practice including:

- ECEC which respects and values the child and stimulates natural curiosity, excitement and desire to learn by doing;

- knowledge of the value of emotional well-being which is influencing practice with children, parents, communities and the ECEC workforce and their trainers;

- practice that is truly inclusive and values children and parents as equal partners;

- a growing understanding of 'non-judgemental' approaches and a philosophy which recognises that we learn by making mistakes and by building on the knowledge of experience;

- an improving understanding of the need for flexibility rather than rigidity in ECEC planning and practice;

- a growing understanding and use of reflection, dialogue and research as tools to explore challenges;

- a growing body of skilful practitioners who understand the complexity and demands of partnership working and who are helping to develop and refine new approaches;

- appropriately trained leadership drawn from a wide range of professions and with diverse perspectives, commited to empower others for the needs of children, families and communities to be served.

These are exciting times and partnership working has a great deal to offer. For it to be successful requires understanding of nature of the demands and processes as the following chapters will show.

☐ Summary

The key points to remember from this chapter are:

- Partnership working is beneficial in addressing the needs of children, families and communities more effectively and efficiently.

- When agencies fail to work together there have been dire consequences.

- Partnership working may mean different things to different agencies.

- The same terms may be used to describe different things causing misunderstanding and frustration.

- The increased interest in the Early Years Education and Childcare agendas has grown with the increased understanding of the importance of ECEC in addressing the long-term consequences of poverty.

- Government priorities for addressing the effects of poverty in the new millennium have created an agenda for more joined-up approaches and moved this forward by funding initiatives and research and facilitating dialogue involving all stakeholders.

- Research has shown the value of partnership working in providing more cohesion between agencies and greater involvement of service users in identifying needs and deciding priorities for services.

- The need for a more skilled and qualified ECEC workforce has led to new qualifications at all levels and a national qualification for integrated centre leadership.

- Leadership is important if partnership working is to be effective and currently draws on a wide range of experience.

Further reading 📖

For a more detailed historical overview the following are very useful:

- Bruce, T. and Meggitt, C. (2002) *Childcare and Education*, 3rd edn. London: Hodder and Stoughton.

- Bruce, T. and Meggitt, C. (2006) *An Introduction to Child Care and Education*, 3rd edn. London: Hodder Arnold. This text provides accessible theory and practical advice.

- Clark, M.M. and Waller, T. (eds) (2007) *Early Childhood Education and Care: Policy and Practice.* London: SAGE.

- Quinton D. (2004) *Supporting Parents: Messages from Research.* London: Jessica Kingsley.

Useful websites

For more detail on the aims, background and organisation of service delivery:

- www.victoria-climbie-inquiry.org.uk

- www.everychildmatters.gov.uk/aims/background/

- www.everychildmatters.gov.uk/deliveringservices/caf/

- www.dcsf.gov.uk/everychildmatters/research/evaluations/nationalevalution/NESS/ness publications/

- www.teachernet.gov.uk/_doc/11184/6937_DFES_Every_Parent_MattersFINAL_PDF_as_ published_130307.pdf

For details of children's centres and Together for Children:

- www.childrens-centres.org/default.aspx

- www.togetherforchildren.co.uk/

For other professional perspectives:

Interprofessional education 1: Definition and drivers –

- www.swap.ac.uk/learning/IPE4.asp

Camden Early Years Intervention Team – www.camden.gov.uk then follow the links to: Education followed by Childcare and Contact the Early Years Team.

2

The models and principles that form the basis of partnership working in practice

This chapter sets out to provide insights into how separate agencies have gradually developed closer working relationships to achieve clearer under-standing and to respond to local needs. 'What partnership working looks like' describes the changes in basic philosophy, aims and principles leading to greater coordination of services, increased consultation between profession-als and other professionals, families and children, and the inclusion of chil-dren, families and communities as more equal partners.

Different models of organisation for multi-agency centres are described showing the variations which developed before children's centres expanded and became a key programme in their own right. The advantages of more 'joined-up' approaches are described. The practical implications of emerging partnership working are explored using examples from leaders of children's centres who in turn represent a wide range of professional backgrounds and perspectives. Consideration is then given to the benefits of increased partner-ship and the practical implications for children, families and communities. There is consideration of available services and what this in turn means for local authorities and partner agencies.

The chapter concludes with further practitioner perspectives on part-nership working leading into a reflection on how partnership working within ECEC works.

What does partnership working look like?

In many ways the basic philosophy of partnership working is not new. The notion of different teams, each with specific tasks combining to achieve together some-thing far greater than they could alone, goes back to the hunter-gatherer commu-nities of earliest history. Military and civil success has also depended on the organisation and development of team skills and leadership. In pre-industrial com-munities the different skills provided by individuals or small groups enabled the whole community to thrive and benefit. The industrial and post-industrial ages have given birth to a gradual increase in our understanding of how the different ways of mixing skills, managing processes and leading teams as a combined whole works, and how this can be developed and improved. In each of these examples through history the way the team members combined was determined by individual and group needs and the social organisations the members lived in.

During the last century western society moved from the form and order of industrially based communities to more flexible working and living conditions as economies became more global. The new century has brought the challenges of rapid change and a need for more flexible working and living with far less certainty of direction or continuity of action.

The effect on Early Childhood Education and Care (ECEC) has been both economic and practical. Within the UK new priorities have been set by the government to address poverty and make better use of the potential workforce, to enable more women to have equal access to employment and to return to work more quickly after starting a family, and to improve levels of education for all. This has led to agendas where high-quality education and care and community development are key aspects.

Where previously agencies working with communities and families did so separately, there has been a move towards more 'joined-up thinking'. This emphasis by the government has led to a move away from 'silo' mentalities to more partnership working and Children's Centres have developed as a key element of the new vision in practice.

Figure 2.1 illustrates how the separation of services worked previously.

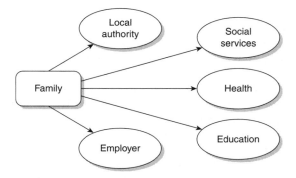

Figure 2.1   Former separation of families and agencies

While cooperation and communication previously existed, essentially the agencies were separate, with the local authority as the key provider and organiser. The boundaries within and between what was provided meant that to achieve one task, service users often had to relate to more than one organisation or department individually, telling their story and providing their personal information several times over. In this climate it required great persistence for families and communities to access services, and when they did agencies themselves reflected separation internally:

- Local authority departments might have had desks next to each other in the same room but the individuals did not necessarily speak to each other.

- Schools tended to communicate mainly with others in the same high school pyramid or sector (primary or secondary) but rarely across sectors.

- Different health departments kept hard-copy records, which *they* owned rather than the patient, on their separate sites and did not always share information with other departments or patients, or if they did there were delays while the paper records were physically passed on.

- Social services were a relatively new phenomenon in the process of establishing their own identity and were often feared by families in communities, particularly as they held rights of access not held by other agencies, combined with powers to remove children.

The organisations tended to be hierarchical and to treat individuals and families with a distanced, professional detachment.

Activity

Find out what systems existed before IT technology was available: how were records kept and who kept them?

What implications did this have on practice?

What message did this give to service users?

What effect did this have on service users?

How has this changed or improved?

Over time communication and cooperation increased between agencies, between schools themselves, between Health, Education and Social Services, particularly in working together at case conferences trying to assist children and families in need, and between school and Health services, where the school nurse and school doctor were invaluable partners in the 1980s and 1990s leading in part to establishing earlier identification and greater inclusion for children with Special Needs in schools. Cooperation between agencies involved in Special Needs led the way in terms of partnership working and in joining up services working around children, families and communities. The position of children and their rights has been strengthened by successive Acts of Parliament (see Thomas, 2004).

This gradual change and shift in emphasis became a paradigm shift with the New Labour government from 1997 onwards. A fresh approach encouraged organisations to re-examine their philosophy and practice to increase cooperation and move towards coordination, to move away from hierarchy to more egalitarian approaches, to be inclusive rather than exclusive and, critically, to put children and families first. This change mirrored changes in Europe and the wider world.

Dahlberg et al. (1999: ch.1) identified the effects of this paradigm shift and called for a reappraisal of the fundamental values and ethics underlying change to include wider perspectives, particularly those involved in the consideration of 'quality'. They argued for more critical examination by asking much deeper questions, including reflection on process rather than on the superficial effects and narrow outcomes.

Points for reflection

Dahlberg et al. (1999: 5–6) identify the following issues emerging from writers in the 1990s when considering quality:

> the *process* of defining quality – who is involved and how it is done ... the understanding that quality is a *subjective, value based, relative* and *dynamic* concept, with the possibility of *multiple perspectives* or understandings ... work on quality needs to be *contextualized*. (original italics)

What would these changes of perception demand of organisations and individuals?

What would help or hinder these changes?

The new vision already existed, developed from family centres run by Social Services, nursery schools with far-sighted leaders who developed family-based approaches and settings such as the original eight which were included in the pilot phase of the Early Excellence Centre programme. These eight, which expanded to eleven in the first year, provided starting points and potential models of good practice. Bertram et al. (2002) identified three basic types of organisation: the 'Unified Model', the 'Coordinated Model' and the 'Coalition Model'. These identified organisational structures similar to those described in Chapter 1. The first describes settings where practice is fully integrated with leadership and management, which may include service delivery by different agencies but is essentially planned, delivered and reviewed as a unified whole. The second describes cooperative working but where each agency or unit retains responsibility for functions related to their areas of skill or expertise, normally under separate leadership and management, yet working in collaboration with a management team made up of representatives from each constituent part. The third is where 'management, training and staffing structures of the services work in a federated partnership', under the leadership of an appointed facilitator or coordinator, yet where each agency is quite separate (Bertram et al., 2002: 40). A further 'Hybrid Model' was added in the following year's report, to describe organisations combining features of some or all of the others described above. The aim in each case was to put the child, family and community at the centre and to operate in a more coordinated way to make services more accessible and to reduce frustration, duplication and costs. Figure 2.2 shows the new vision.

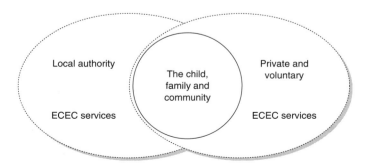

Figure 2.2   New models of organisation

A further model which has become more popular is a 'hub and spokes' model with a main setting at the centre and smaller outreach sites in locations spread around the working area. The setting at the centre is often a phase 1 children's centre or former Sure Start centre which has become a designated children's centre, and the leadership is often a single leader with responsibility for the whole, supported by senior practitioners responsible for the day-to-day running of each separate site. The outposts can provide some of the same core services but in addition offer different services primarily but not exclusively to the local community. The coverage for each centre or cluster tends to follow local authority wards which may well include more than one GP or health centre, midwife or health visitor. A setting will almost certainly cover the catchment areas of more than one school. Even where a setting is sited within the grounds of a single school and where governance is provided by the school, the setting has a duty to relate equally to all the schools in its designated area. The issues around centres on school sites are explored in more depth in Chapter 5.

The new model way of working has taken the best from previous good practice. It is both logical and challenging: logical in that there is access to a wide range of services in the same location – a 'one-stop shop' approach (see Chapter 5); challenging because the model is developing from services designed to function in their own way and from their own perspective, where cooperation has tended to mean 'others cooperating with us'. It is also not *all* services together. Initially 'key services' were grouped from existing agencies, but it rapidly became clear that a better model was to go into the communities and find out what was wanted by members of the community rather than administrators deciding what was needed or best for them. Understanding this is key to understanding the underpinning philosophy and practice: the agencies are there to meet the needs of the clients as individuals, families and groups who are equal partners.

Note: the children's centre programme was introduced in phases: phase 1 centres between 2004-5 and 2006 were well funded and either purpose built or adaptations of school or other public, private or independently owned buildings, phase 2 aimed to increase numbers by 2,500 new centres between 2006 and 2008 and phase 3 had the longer term aim of 3,500 additional centres by 2010 'one for every community' Phases 2 and 3 received less overall funding and tended to be less frequently purpose built with many Local Authorities opting for phase 3 centers to be much smaller and buying in service provision off site as well as on. For more information see www/dcsf.gov.uk/everychildmatters/earlyyears/surestart/aboutsurestart/about surestart

What does this mean in practice?

Some leaders of children's centres when asked to describe what they saw as 'multi-agency or partnership working' responded as follows:

> A collaborative professional working relationship with others in both the professional and para-professional world of all agencies who work jointly to deliver services to local children and families. I also consider this to mean a partnership with parents and their children to deliver services in consultation with them to address their needs.

This response captures the essence of children's centres which bring together a wide range of professionals to meet the needs of children, parents and communities as defined by them themselves, as well as those identified by different professional and para-professional agencies.

> Several agencies with their own professionalisms working together to deliver a shared service.

> Three principal agencies: education, health, and social care.

> Different professionals from diverse backgrounds coming together for a common purpose ...

These three responses suggest acknowledgement of and emphasis on the importance of the skills, perspectives and attitudes each agency can bring to bear when considering the needs of individuals and families. There is an unspoken implication here of the enabling role of the children's centre in drawing agencies together to identify needs, points of contact and both short- and long-term support and to act in a facilitating role. There is also a monitoring and review role to ensure necessary changes are seen and acted upon and to listen to all those involved. Support may well be needed for the individuals representing the agencies as much as for those receiving help and support from the agencies.

> A strong team working together to offer the inclusive and quality services that families want and need.

This response indicates the importance of the children's centre's internal team and the wider partnership team. A strong team requires commitment and understanding, trust and confidence among and between team members. It requires effective leadership with clear vision and beliefs which are communicated to the wider team. Equally important is the knowledge and appropriate use of a range of leadership styles. All of this takes time to develop and establish and constant attention to renew and extend.

> Professionals working together to provide services in order to meet ECM outcomes.

This comment acknowledges the statutory requirements which apply to those working in children's centres. These seem to be very clear but different professions may well perceive these requirements in different ways or with subtly different interpretations or emphases. This will affect the internal and wider teams and how they approach issues. It is also affected by the understanding all involved have of the Early Years Foundation Stage (EYFS) and changes within professions, such as Education and the new Early Years Professional Status (EYPS) qualification (see Chapter 5).

 Activity

Make a list of:

- enabling factors that encourage individuals from diverse professional backgrounds to work towards becoming an effective team;
- barriers to developing multi-agency teams within children's centres;
- attributes that will make successful multi-agency leaders.

Relating and working collectively with more than one other agency to provide an 'individual package of care' for a family.

Missed opportunities for other agencies that are resistant to work in a similar way to us. Frustrations when trying to coordinate meetings (non-attendance).

These two statements illustrate very different perspectives. The first, optimistic in tone, describes the aim of partnership working and points to a belief that partnership working can happen. The second acknowledges the frustration which can arise when reality gets in the way of partnership working. It is very important to maintain a realistic view of partnership working. It is not something that is normally easy to achieve. It does require careful preparation and may well need a step-by-step approach. Partners often need to be convinced of the likely gains before committing themselves to new ways of working. The new partnership may well mean that partner agencies have to reconcile current practices and issues such as confidentiality may need careful negotiation. The following quotations show what can be achieved when these barriers are overcome:

The fantastic turnout of staff from a whole range of agencies who come to events for families on Saturdays and muck in to help the whole thing run smoothly.

Teams of professionals working in partnership to enable families to receive seamless services.

Lots of different people from different backgrounds working together on a project/ piece of work etc.

The way in which partner agencies combine in a planned and considered way is suggested in the following examples:

Lots of agencies working together under one roof with a shared vision and purpose.

Core values of a team that understand each other and work side by side to complement each other's profession.

Key agencies with similar responsibilities coming together to plan so that duplication is avoided and the process of working together enhances the capacity to deliver services to children and parents.

The parents, carers, voluntary and statutory services working together to deliver services for children and families ...

It is not possible to have 'a shared vision and purpose' or team 'core values' unless there has been a conscious exchange of ideas within a setting or in terms of the wider partner agencies (Rummery, 2003: 214; Aubrey, 2008: 92). This really needs to take place as early as possible within the life of any partnership. Where this is achieved it often enables a clear set of parameters and 'ground rules' to be established as protocols. It also helps to allay fears and avoid misunderstandings. The second quotation above suggests that not only can greater efficiency be achieved but that the process of planning and consultation enhances the capabilities and understandings of those taking part. This is particularly important in easing people towards a more cooperative frame of mind and helping all involved to understand the non-judgemental basis of discussions. Discussing the known and safe areas around practical issues can help all to feel more at ease and to understand each other better, before more complex areas are tackled and the status described in the third example above can be achieved.

Not all the responses were unqualified or entirely positive. The following two show reservations:

I think of our SSLP [Sure Start Local Programme] in its heyday.

More than one agency working together to try and achieve specific outcomes. However, multi-agency working tends to mean something enforced upon you and for me is done at the exclusion of clients (top-down). Partnership working I feel is more about involving clients.

The first seems to suggest that what the centre leader had experienced previously in their SSLP is the first thing to come to mind when they think of partnership working. It is not clear if this means partnership working is not now happening, is on a par with their previous experience or if this means their previous experience was especially good for some reason. What this does show is that successful partnership working does need to be constantly nurtured and cared for if it is to develop and improve. Achieving success does not mean anything can be taken for granted. The second comment shows the importance of ensuring that practice matches values and aims and also reinforces the need to maintain partnerships as carefully as any other sophisticated mechanism.

The final group of comments captures the sense of excitement and the opportunities that open up when partnership working is enabled:

> True exciting possibilities of being able to ensure professionals are able to work together to support the delivery of outcomes irrespective of their employing body or professional background.

> Huge meetings with lots of people sitting round a table sharing information!

> Agencies coming into the centre to deliver their services ...

> Opportunities!! ...

The vast majority of these comments are positive and illustrate the excitement and challenge involved. However, there are also frustrations. Some of the barriers and limitations are explored below and are visited again more fully in Chapter 6.

 Points for reflection

> Many partners are used to working in their own way: what will partnership working demand from staff from all agencies?

> What will successful partnership require of leaders?

> What will this require from administrators at all levels?

How does this work with children?

There is a balance between identifying emotional and social needs, developmental (health) needs and cognitive (educational) needs. Children's centres themselves are designed to be child friendly and encourage participation. Children have been consulted in the arrangement of resources and decor. The Children's Commissioner set up the '11 Million' project to encourage children and young people to express their views on what they like and what they want in life. The organisation website provides an opportunity to give and receive information in a child-friendly way. The website is also linked to pilot programmes in England based at children's centres. Essentially it provides a mouthpiece for children so that their views are heard. One method used in the '11 Million' project (www.11million.org.uk/) was to provide disposable cameras and children were asked to take pictures of what was important in their lives. The images have provided a collage which gives insights into how the children perceive their lives. Some children's centres have used the project to find out what children like and dislike and have then been able to investigate why the unpopular areas and aspects were so and how they could be adjusted and improved. In one particular setting this experience led to staff bringing colour swatches for the children to select colours they liked so that they grey steel railings could be made more attractive. A similar technique was used in a children's hospital and staff were surprised at the ceiling of the anaesthetic room featuring prominently in the dislikes. The children said this was because it was clinical and lacking decoration, and it was what the children were looking at as they went into anaesthetic. The children suggested ways of improving it and action was taken to make the ceiling more attractive.

Children's centres, Sure Start centres and other partnership working environments have improved in design. More consideration is given to how rooms are likely to be used. More attention is given to seeking design ideas from families and children. This could be improved further: some basic designs include windows that are too high, there is little imagination used in floor surfaces and furnishings and even creative outdoor areas tend to become copies of others rather than unique. It takes imagination and a degree of risk but innovation is possible as the case study below demonstrates.

 Case study

Creative structural changes in a nursery school in Southern Germany where a standard red-brick, single-storey, 1950s building had been transformed.

The normally flat windows have been changed and extended outwards on a triangular base with two floor-to-ceiling windows, creating a bay inside the room and also outside. Outside the jutting windows created bays each with a defined theme such as a beach, a tropical area with bamboos and tall grasses, water features, a bird garden.

The inside space has allowed the construction of a two-storey wooden house, with slightly different designs in different rooms. Each has a lower playroom space and a circular staircase leading to an upper room and platform providing a bird's eye view of the classroom. There is also a raised section in each of the rooms across corners to provide different perspectives for the children. The multi-purpose furniture, designed in curves rather than rectangles, can be fitted together to provide a bendy table for the whole group or used separately in smaller interestingly shaped units. The cost was within the budget allowed for renovation but has provided a much more interesting and stimulating context for children's lives.

Genuine partnership between agencies can mean that efforts are coordinated and focused from design through to practice and are empowering for children. Children have access to experiences and equipment that encourage them to explore, connect and make meaning (Bertram et al., 2006). Research has shown how important emotional stability is for young children (see the High/Scope Perry Preschool Study discussed by Schweinhart et al., 1993, 2004) and the beneficial effects of a secure start to later confidence in adult life. In partnership working and children's centres, children relate to a consistent group of adults and have access to high-quality care and education and additional support if needed in familiar surroundings. The staff need to have understanding of developmental, health, well-being and educational charac-teristics and be in tune with the aims and services of the whole centre. The staff also have to be able to engage with parents sensitively and from the same value base as staff from their own and all other centres (see also agency providers in Chapter 4).

How does this work for parents?

Parents are able to seek advice, support and help from specialist agencies such as Homestart and Job Centre Plus as well as financial management advice and health services including breast feeding, first aid and counselling and support services. They can begin to improve their own learning in personal and domestic life skills, parent-ing skills, healthy eating, IT, literacy and numeracy, health and safety at home, and recreational and therapeutic activities such as fitness and creative arts. The advan-tage is that the services are suggested by parents, take place in small groups, are non-threatening, progress at a pace to suit those attending, are sensitive to issues of inclusion and take place in familiar surroundings and with familiar staff.

Staff from centres go into communities and actively make contact with individu-als. Existing service users are encouraged to bring others to outreach groups, 'drop-in' sessions or 'taster' sessions. Centre staff aim to help parents grow in confidence and self-esteem and to begin to take ownership of their lives. In many cases centre staff and parents work together on specific projects and longer-term planning.

 Case study

Empowering young mothers through a South Wales Sure Start

A visit to a Sure Start programme in South Wales enabled a meeting with a group of young mothers who described how their lives had been turned round by the care and encouragement they had received from the setting staff. Before Sure Start set up the site, the young women had felt trapped in their homes with their children. There were no local amenities so even the most basic needs required an effort.

A member of the outreach staff made contact with individuals initially to find out what activities or services they would like to have locally and when a small group began attending stay and play sessions they found they were not alone and began to build confidence. They were asked what they would like to do and the staff then arranged short programmes to do with health, care and cooking. The children could be left in a separate crèche room on the same site while the parents had time and space to focus on the theme. They felt less stressed and less trapped, better able to see what they wanted and had the courage to ask for it. They now have a self-help group and actively encourage others to make use of the facilities by word of mouth and poster campaigns. The staff team leader drew on contacts with local midwives and health visitors and was able to draw on a range of additional staff skills to work with the young mothers by unobtru-sively contributing to the parent and baby and parent and toddler sessions.

This kind of working requires staff who are attentive and who actively listen, who look beyond the immediate needs of their specialist skills and who are aware of their colleagues' knowledge and skill areas so that parents' needs can be identified, prioritised and addressed sensitively and in partnership with colleagues from other agencies. This kind of working demands a willingness to work in combination with different emphases at different times, and with appropriate agencies taking the lead as the current agreed focus demands a high degree of flexibility is therefore required and structures that are less hierarchical. It also demands staff who are able to work alongside parents and colleagues yet are able to use their own initiative.

The process of outreach varies with each local authority and the phase of development of any given centre. Many settings have a designated outreach worker or team while others use existing contacts, for example through health visitors or midwives. The outreach role enables contact with individuals and groups within the setting area, helps to make them aware of what is already available and encourages a discussion of what they as individuals might wish for in addition. Settings run open days and fun events which promote their activities and extend their contacts with the children, families and the community.

 Activity

Find out what provision exists for families and children in your local area.

What are the benefits of partnership working for local families and children?

What are the limitations?

How could these be overcome?

How can professional agencies begin to empower parents more successfully?

How does this work for families?

Partnership working provides access for families to services that they want at a local centre and contact with known and trusted staff with whom they can build relationships that are supportive and empowering. Figure 2.3 provides a diagrammatic example which illustrates how this can begin to work in practice.

In this example there are different possible pathways for an initial contact – through an outreach worker, the midwife or the key worker for either child – or it could be that the parent comes to the setting with a friend or for a different initial purpose. Setting staff see families as a whole, while also attending to individual needs. Outreach workers make initial contact and each member of the family is encouraged to build a relationship with one or more staff to whom they can turn for help and advice. Staff take a long-term view, working to help family members solve their own issues, rather than providing 'quick-fix' solutions or solving the issues for them.

Many settings have drop-in facilities, 'stay and play' sessions, internet cafés, crèches and playgroups which may be run by other providers, in partnership with setting leadership and management. Members of families can meet with others, undertake skills training and have access to advice, counselling, advocacy and employment information.

Figure 2.3 illustrates the potential points of contact through the midwife to introduce the children's centre to the mother who will then have a key worker to relate to. As

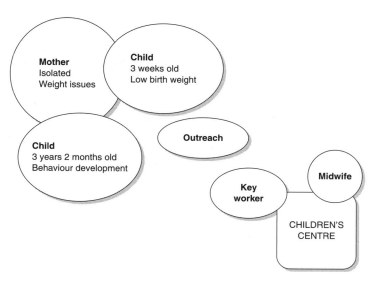

Figure 2.3   Potential points of contact through outreach

other agencies become involved a lead professional will coordinate the involvement and any action decided in consultation with the parent.

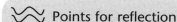 Points for reflection

Which other agencies might be included in such an example?

What factors should influence who is the lead professional?

How does it work for communities?

Many of the advantages which apply for individuals and families are also there for the wider community. In addition many settings have rooms which can be hired and services that benefit all, such as Job Centre Plus or financial management services. Many of the training and adult learning programmes are open to the whole community, not just families with pre-school children.

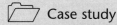 Case study

St Thomas Centre Community Hall

The St Thomas Centre in Birmingham was converted from a 1960s secondary school in partnership with the community association, city authority and DfES. The transition took time, with the nursery on site for several years before other services began to share the building. The first phase of building refurbishment

(Continued)

> work was funded by the Early Excellence Centre programme and provided new and refurbished accommodation for the nursery, new administration rooms and additional rooms for partner agencies such as the city 'Flying Start' team. The second phase of new building and extension was paid for by the community association, Birmingham Children's Services and the centre itself. A significant part of this was the conversion of the former school gym, housed in a first-floor room above the nursery with separate access. It now has movable, tiered seating, screen and projection facilities, and a kitchen. It is a multi-function room available to the community and to agencies. The hall provides accessible facilities for the newly developed Attwood Green housing park.

Many settings are developing trust and enabling more open access to centre facilities. Cafe areas are proving to be a popular innovation and as well as offering informal peer support and initial points of contact with staff or service providers, work well as dropin areas and locations for breast feeding support often providing internet access and information services. Partnerships with families and the wider community served by each centre are being developed successfully in many areas as the illustrations show, although there is a need for this to remain an active aim constantly under review.

What services are available?

The Sure Start Children's Centres website lists the following core areas:

These services vary according to centre but may include:

- integrated early education and childcare – all centres offering Early Years provision have a minimum half-time qualified teacher (increasing to full-time within 18 months of the centre opening)
- support for parents – including advice on parenting, local childcare options and access to specialist services for families
- child and family health services – ranging from health screening, health visitor services to breast-feeding support
- helping parents into work – with links to the local Jobcentre Plus and training.

(www.surestart.gov.uk)

The range of partners can be extensive and is explored more fully in Chapter 4. The extent of partnership is implicit in the 'core offer', where provision of services for children under 5 and their families includes:

- early education and day care, including the identification of children with additional needs, which requires working closely with statutory and independent health and care agencies;

- outreach to parents, including parents with additional needs, which requires working in partnership with support workers for ethnic minorities, health and social services;

- health services, which includes working with midwives, health visitors, GPs and respite care providers.

The core offer also specifies the provision of support, a base for childminders and a service hub for parents and providers of childcare services which potentially opens doors to other working partnerships. In addition there is an expectation of links with Jobcentre Plus and local training providers for further and higher education institutions and management and workforce training, and effective links with nurseries, including Neighbourhood Nurseries, and schools, including out of school clubs and extended schools. All of this requires the establishment of sound working relationships with a bewildering range of other agencies. The leadership implications are significant and are explored more fully in Chapter 7.

What does this mean for local authorities and agencies?

Without real partnerships children's centres cannot meet their core offer. The underpinning philosophy and values, combined with the organisational demands, represent a considerable challenge to local authorities and agencies. The philosophy and values are based on a vision of service that puts the child, the family and the community at the centre, as shown by the following example from Camden.

Aims of the Camden Family Support Model

- Early identification and assessment of child and family needs
- Link to specialist services
- Link to drop-in services
- Gateway to information, advice, training and appropriate onward referral
- Promote early education
- Encourage parents in accessing training employment and childcare
- Alter parental perceptions and isolation by supporting involvement in community life by facilitating and supporting parent forums and other community-based activities
- Commitment to sharing professional knowledge and working together professionally to develop an integrated approach within the service and outwards to other agencies.

(Houston and Houston, 2006)

This evaluation was very positive and provides indications for maintaining the success of a developing partnership. However, this contrasts with many other cases where practice has tended to work differently. Service planning and delivery has tended to be top-down and on the basis of services that were deemed to be required. While this may have included market research there was little doubt who made the decisions. Organisation has tended to suit the providing agency, whether it be the local authority or other. This has been the case where outside expertise or service delivery has been bought in by the local authority, or imposed, e.g. by external agencies taking over the provision of education services when local authorities have failed Ofsted inspections. In the latter case the agencies do not see consultation as any part of their remit. The previous lack of flexibility or response to need has led to the growth of non-statutory, private and independent agencies which have tried to fill the gaps left in statutory provision (see the list above).

Points for reflection

In the services listed by the children's centre leaders which are statutory and which are non-statutory and independent bodies?

In the UK what other non-statutory bodies might be included?

What implications does partnership working have for local authorities and for other agencies?

The nature of the challenge is explored in more detail in Chapter 6. A key aspect is the institutional ethos and heritage, the mindset of the organisation, its leaders and employees. This is difficult to change and adapt to the demands for flexibility and a bottom-up approach, which is at the heart of successful partnership working. It is also influenced by the political tone of the local authority in particular as well as the views of those who hold power at each level of the administration. Good intentions and stated policy on their own are not enough to achieve successful partnership working and a lack of real commitment from key sections of the administration can block deep commitment from others and frustrate months of hard negotiation. Each agency has to be given a sound reason to join in this way of working if they are really to be whole-heartedly committed. Commitment then has to be nurtured and maintained: it can never be assumed or taken for granted.

How do practitioners see partnership working?

When researching material for this chapter I had intended to seek the views of practitioners from different professional heritages in order to draw out similarities and differences. What I discovered was that while there are differences in perspective these are not barriers to those already committed to partnership working. Indeed the differences are used positively to enrich partnerships and creative approaches. What became clear was that committed practitioners from different backgrounds have similar views as to the most important aspects that contribute to building partnerships. Among these, clear aims, good relationships and trust are seen as key with an overwhelming emphasis on good relationships that are open, honest and respectful and develop trust (Aubrey, 2008: 169–170; Anning et al., 2006: ch. 8). The interpersonal aspects seem to come before almost any other consideration and can overcome the hierarchy and established protocols and procedures. Children's centre leaders stress the importance of having clear, shared aims and protocols and clear vision, and they emphasise the value of being positive, focused and creative. There is a recognition that success is limited without support from senior managers and that communication at all levels has to be maintained, but they also stress the need to keep a clear focus on children and families equally and not to lose sight of their centrality to everything. Additional attitudes and attributes which feature strongly include respectful listening, consistency, flexibility and a willingness to 'go the extra mile', as well as aspects such as the quality of leadership, the diversity of teams and having a suitable and accessible venue.

In terms of barriers encountered by children's centre leaders the most common factor appears to be fear of change and resistance to change. This works at all levels. Fear undermines staff confidence and morale and extends to the administration and senior officers within local authorities. By definition people are reluctant to leave their comfort zones or tried and tested pathways and procedures. This is even more acute where there is an implicit or explicit contradiction, such as has occurred over financial protocols when Sure Start and other settings have been moved under the administration of Education, or when children's centres are located on school sites while serving a much wider area than the school catchment. Allied to this is poor communication and lack of management support or ineffective management, and a reluctance to break barriers. This is often exacerbated by changes in personnel which damage continuity and consistency in approach. In some cases cost-saving has led to responsibilities being added to portfolios of individuals who are already overloaded or who have no knowledge of the ECEC agenda.

Children's centre leaders have encountered opposition that has arisen from possessiveness and a rigid view of professional boundaries which creates an overwhelmingly negative attitude. The attitudes displayed by those with whom they have to work can include arrogance from individuals and organisational cultures and behaviour which amounts to bullying. As representatives of new approaches and champions of innovation, children's centre leaders have to confront outdated practices, red tape and bureaucracy and are by definition flying in the face of convention. It is hardly surprising that their approaches are often misunderstood and even resented.

Many leaders are constrained by lack of time and staffing restrictions. There are inconsistencies nationally in resourcing while the core offer remains the same: some local authorities have used a minimalist model when setting up phase 2 children's centres with a centre leader, an administrative officer and one other member of staff, where as others have greater allocations for essentially the same remit. In such circumstances a newly promoted centre leader faces real difficulties when they find themselves on a school site with a headteacher as line manager and under the governance of the school governing body, when neither has an understanding of the purpose or reach of the centre or of the philosophy underpinning its approach to service users. This is not helped when combined with funding issues, lack of understanding of purpose and reach and overall lack of clear objectives. This is explored further in Chapter 6.

What is clear is the importance of the awareness of practitioners who are committed to the new model, irrespective of professional heritage, of the nutrients and toxins which are involved in successful partnership working.

How does this work within early childhood education and care?

Early childhood care and education services are now more commonly grouped within local authority Children's Services but there are variations across the UK. There is more emphasis on 'joined-up thinking' and the incentives are more positive in supporting moves to enable greater partnership working, for example the Common Assessment Framework (CAF) which is based in partnership working. However, many departments and agencies are struggling to balance their current demands under the existing systems, protocols and habits. Trying to create new mindsets and systems is very difficult to achieve in practice. In some cases local reorganisation means that there are changes in personnel and job specification which do not always accommodate the partnership vision, or if they do, the turmoil of the process of internal change disables any other initiatives. In all of this, funding is a key element.

Funding is a thorny issue. Quite rightly local authorities and agencies have careful accounting and fiscal procedures. Auditors conduct regular checks on accounts and have a duty to report inadequate or inappropriate procedures. In cases where breaches of procedure are deemed to have occurred, the individual responsible, usually the head or leader, can be suspended while formal investigations are made. Because of this any financial creativity has to be within the current rules in force. While this is absolutely right and proper, it does mean that settings which are by definition innovative and searching for new ways of addressing funding solutions need to take great care to remain within legal limits. The danger is that the vision of the children's centre may not be shared by financial administrators whose training and mode of working is focused on keeping within procedures rather than finding ways to extend or adapt them. This is a very real dilemma at the heart of what partnership working is about. This is explored further in Chapter 5.

Key elements for successful partnership working

The children's centre leaders consulted clarified the key elements for successful partnership working as being grounded in shared values and visions strengthened by the following principles:

- All those involved are valued, differing perspectives are respected, and skills, training and experience contribute collectively.

- Change comes from the bottom up rather than top down.

- Services need to be brought to the community rather than the reverse and accessibility improved.

- Services need to be co-located to improve coordination of services.

- More open access to training and skills is required.

- Highest priority should be given to areas of highest need.

- Causes rather than effects need to be addressed.

- There needs to be greater development of services such as advocacy to provide a voice for the vulnerable.

- Support which builds towards independence rather than dependency needs to be developed.

- There needs to be more emphasis on improving self-esteem and self-worth.

- There needs to be more encouragement of non-judgemental working.

- High-quality pre-school care and education provision must be a priority supported by the employment of part-time teachers and inspection.

In addition professionals need attitudes that value and foster:

- open mindedness – moving away from the all-knowing expert professional stance;

- the development of trust;

- adaptability and flexibility;

- the development of support which builds towards independence rather than dependency;

- the development of leadership that encourages flat hierarchies and distributed leadership (Hargreaves, 2006: 82);

- actively working to include all the stakeholders as equal partners.

How this works in practice is the subject of Chapter 3.

Summary

The key points to remember from this chapter are:

- Partnership involves all stakeholders as equals and reflects the 'flat hierarchies' that underpin children's centre leadership.

- Successful partnership working requires a shared vision, clear communication, commitment, creativity, flexibility, support from leadership at all levels and realistic funding.

- Values are shared by all and underpin organisation and practice.

- Partnership working allows greater unity of service provision.

- Services are designed to match needs identified by the communities, families and individuals.

- There are barriers embedded in separate agencies and their preferred ways of working that need to be overcome for partnership working to be successful.

- The attitudes of potential partners are key to success.

Further reading

The following provide useful information about partnership working in theory and practice:

- Anning, A. and Ball, M. (2008) *Improving Services for Young Children: From Sure Start to Children's Centres.* London: SAGE.

- Maynard, T. and Thomas, N. (eds) (2008) *An Introduction to Early Childhood Studies.* London: SAGE.

Useful websites

How child-centred approaches have moved on and been developed in more recent policy can be found at:

- www.everychildmatters.gov.uk/aims/background/

- www.everychildmatters.gov.uk/aims/childrenstrusts/

- www.dfes.gov.uk/publications/childrensplan/downloads/The_Childrens_Plan.pdf (Introduction by Ed Balls, Secretary of State for Children, Schools and Families)

More examples from practice can be found at:

- www.childrens-centres.org/Topics/FAQ/CCFAQ.aspx

Details of the Children's Commissioner can be found at:

- www.11million.org.uk/

3

Developments in partnership working

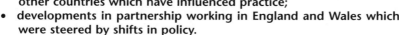

The two previous chapters have introduced what partnership is, where it has come from and the principles of how it works. This chapter looks at influences on the development of partnership working from two sources:

- developments in partnership working using three case studies from other countries which have influenced practice;
- developments in partnership working in England and Wales which were steered by shifts in policy.

Examples from other countries which have influenced practice

The last 25 years have seen Early Years practitioners developing dialogue and exchanging information about practice within their own countries and increasingly internationally. The rapid changes in communication have helped to make this possible. Greater availability of travel has enabled practitioners to visit other locations and learn first-hand in ways that were not possible previously and there has been positive encouragement by incentives supported by the government and the British Council, such as the Comenius project and other initiatives from the European Union. This has led to an increase in shared knowledge and wider understanding, and more recently there has been a growing focus of interest on specific examples of innovative practice.

The three selected case studies will be familiar to many practitioners in Early Childhood Education and Care (ECEC) and many will have been influenced by the pioneering practice represented by the Forest Schools of Denmark, the example of Reggio Emilia, Italy and Te Whaariki in New Zealand. The aim of using these examples here is to illustrate common features of partnership working and to underline its potential, rather to explore the detail of the good practice which they represent. While the effects of these three examples have been significant in inspiring a wider international audience and affecting practice not only in the UK but worldwide, nevertheless the creative innovations they provide are deeply rooted in the cultures of the countries that produced them and the prevailing domestic political climates.

What these examples have to teach us about the combination of social, political and practical partnership working is the main focus of this chapter.

The Forest Schools of Denmark

Forest Schools provide pre-school children with opportunities to explore their natural surroundings and interact with each other and the natural environment. The adults facilitate the exploration providing support and encouragement, stimulating discussion and debate and helping children to develop a sense of their own well-being as well as the well-being of their companions.

In Scandinavian countries there is a collective community responsibility taken for the education and care of children. They have the lowest rates of child poverty in the world according to UNICEF (2005) and childhood has traditionally been viewed as a unique, distinct and separate phase of life, not simply a preparation for school. This belief in childhood means high taxation is acceptable and helps to pay for high-quality services, including subsidised early education and care for all. The strong belief in the family unit accounts for generous maternity and paternity leave enabling families to establish attachment and a secure start for their children. In Denmark, as in other Scandinavian countries, partnership working is grounded in the tradition of dialogue and consultation and has developed to include greater strategic collaboration and coordination between settings, parents, local and national politicians and administrators. There are differences between individual Scandinavian countries (see OECD, 2006a) but essentially partnership working is embedded in the culture and enables high-quality services to be provided for all children from age 2. The example provided by Denmark and the Scandinavian countries generally is in a shared value base which is translated into practice through generous funding to provide high-quality ECEC experiences.

In Denmark, pre-school experiences are largely practical and encourage personal and social development, exploration and meaning-making, before entry into 'Transition' at age 6, the step into the formal, structured education system. There is an emphasis on outdoor activities which are child-led with pedagogues acting as companions on a journey of exploration, which is how the Forest Schools came into being. The principles of Forest Schools have been adopted and become a feature of pre-school and early years in many areas of England and have encouraged the emphasis on outdoor learning and play in England and Wales. It has taken time for the initiative, which was brought to England at the end of the 1990s, to become established and its success has partly been due to the parallel development in the general understanding of the value of outdoor play and activity. The development has required varying degrees of partnership which the following case study illustrates.

 Case study

Bridgwater College

Bridgwater College in Somerset developed an accredited programme to train leaders in Forest School in partnership with the children's centre on site to establish a working example. Parents were involved from an early stage and the partnership extended to include a landowner who agreed to provide a suitable location. The local authority supported the development to extend to other pre-school and early years settings.

Activity

How does Forest School work in England?

Find out what the principles are.

What would it take to plan and organise a Forest School?

What would be the challenges?

What would be the benefits?

Forest Schools are now widely established and the website provides more information (see Useful websites at the end of the chapter).

Reggio Emilia

Reggio Emilia is a municipality in Northern Italy. The pre-schools are organised and run in practice that is grounded in a philosophy developed by Loris Malaguzzi following the end of the Second World War. Essentially the practice is child-centred and recognises the value of creative and imaginative experiences, with the children leading and taking responsibility for their learning.

The example set by Reggio Emilia in Italy is also based in a clear philosophy which is child-centred and which sees the adults as enablers and facilitators of children's development and learning using creative and inspiring approaches. Loris Malaguzzi formulated a philosophy which was influenced by the principles developed by Maria Montessori and his own experiences in post-Second World War Italy. What Malaguzzi and his followers have succeeded in doing is to express their beliefs in practice and to question and reflect, translating their work into a value-based action–reflection cycle which speaks to others in a universal language.

The Reggio approach is an example of principled partnership and collaboration based in research. The programme grew from the destruction and rubble of postwar Italy when several community-run pre-school settings grew up. The initial educational services for the Municipality of Reggio Emilia were set up in 1963 when the first pre-schools were opened for children aged 3 to 6. The community-run settings became part of the developing municipal organisation in 1967. In 1970 this included infant and toddler centres for children aged 3 months to 3 years. The Reggio philosophy and practice evolved into a distinctive, principled system which began to have a national influence and voice in the early 1970s. The international influence developed towards the late 1970s and early 1980s. But the growth and development has not been smooth or untroubled. The very survival of the Reggio system is a tribute to the local partnership, which faced a series of critical attacks from the church and press and serious reductions in funding. These were overcome by the commitment of the administration and the extension of the partnership to include the equivalent of the private and voluntary sector and eventually the Italian Federation of Catholic Pre-schools (FISM). (For further information see the Reggio Children Exhibition Catalogue, 1996: 20.)

Partnerships are essential to the approach: the partnerships are between all the adults, with their skills and training, to meet the needs of children. Adults in this context include the parents, city leaders and administrators, education advisory staff, teachers and artists. The adults' role is to identify and serve the needs of the children and to support their exploration. They achieve this by constantly researching, reflecting on the changes required, and sharing and developing new ways of allowing the children's 'voices' to be heard and expressed. Expression through artistic approaches is fundamental to this process of exploration, discovery and learning. Parents are actively involved, teachers are encouraged to reflect and learn and all children are included, funded by the city and by parents according to their means.

This is a subtle blend of partnership working focused on meeting the needs of children, and therefore families, in a reflexive, adaptable system where all are valued.

Te Whaariki

Te Whaariki is the name given to the changed Early Years curriculum in New Zealand. It is unusual because it came about through partnership working involving the government of New Zealand, specialist pre-school researchers, practitioners, parents, children and communities. The research was significantly influenced by the theories of 'schemas' (Athey, 1990; Nutbrown, 1994).

Partnership between politicians, researchers, practitioners and parents led to a comprehensive national review of New Zealand Early Childhood Education at the start of the millennium. This led to a report in 2001 which provided the basis for a restructuring from basic principles and concepts. Te Whaariki is much more than a curriculum, but draws together social and family-centred strands with those of learning and education, care and welfare, across cultures. The approach to this work was consultative and fully inclusive. The consultation included social and cultural departments and succeeded in blending aims in the process and as an integral part of the outcome. The essence is a focus on strands: well-being, belonging, contribution, communication and exploration. Within these are cultural and learning goals, with practitioners of all professions responsible for facilitating children's learning and development. The process helped to create a more coherent outcome that is understood and supported widely and is a good example of partnership with political leaders working with academics, communities, practitioners and children to achieve a well researched and grounded outcome, addressing health and social as well as educational issues. This represents a highly sophisticated partnership and a concept symbolised by the image of traditional weaving, with the warp and weft representing the cultural and social themes and the ECEC aims and principles.

The three examples discussed above show the interrelationship between social and political contexts and ECEC and their implication for partnership working.

 Points for reflection

What other areas are shared by these examples?

What is needed to achieve the blend of political, social and ECEC priorities illustrated here?

A common feature of the three is the underlying approach to ECEC which these examples demonstrate within these countries. An essential element of this is the belief in early childhood as a distinct and unique stage in human development rather than a preparation for school. A second part is to do with the value of children's connectedness with the whole environment of their home society, and the way in which exploring natural surroundings and phenomena can help children learn about themselves as well as the world around them. A third part is the nature of the society which has produced these initiatives, their strong beliefs in the family unit and their well-defined social values and systems. Lastly, an important common feature is their grounding of practice in philosophy and research, together with partnership with the political climate and leadership.

Dahlberg et al. (1999) point to the fact that those involved in Reggio Emilia pre-schools have never presented their approach as a model to be exported. They have not presented their ideas as a universal 'answer', rather that the methods they have arrived at have worked for them in their particular situation with the children and families they have been working with. The Reggio approach, while encouraging outsiders to re-think their approach, grew from a rejection of fascism and a desire that children should learn to think for themselves. The socialist principles of the municipality underpin the approaches developed. Similarly the researchers, practitioners and politicians of New Zealand do not present Te Whaariki as practice to be copied. They describe the process of partnership working and its benefits for others to critically appraise. Even the Forest Schools have developed from cultural and social beliefs and practices which cannot be transferred. We can certainly learn from the practice and examples of other countries but we need to be aware of what will and what will not transfer.

These examples show how partnership working has affected practice in other countries. They illustrate too how some aspects of partnership working are universal. The next section looks at how changes to promote a shift towards greater partnership working have been encouraged in England and Wales and are developing supported by political initiatives.

Developments in England

In England the explicit provision for partnership working which underpins the government's agenda for change is part of two key documents, *Every Child Matters* (DfES, 2003) and *The Children's Plan* (DCSF, 2007) and is also part of the re-structuring framework set out in the Early Years Foundation Stage.

Every Child Matters

ECM (DfES, 2003) was a government Green Paper heavily influenced by the Laming Report (2003) into the inquiry following the death of Victoria Climbié and the failure of statutory agencies to share information which might have prevented the tragedy. The clear aim was to ensure that the future organisation of child protection provision would:

- concentrate on prevention rather than cure;

- create more effective systems for recognising need and for early intervention that would be effective;

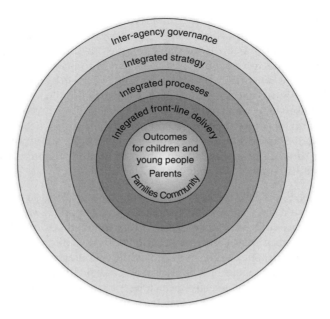

Figure 3.1   'Onion' diagram showing how services should be layered
Source: DfES (2004: 6).

- set in place reforms hinged on greater sharing of information between agencies. This was followed by *Every Child Matters: Next Steps* and the Children Act 2004 which set out in more detail how these changes should be brought about:

   ... providing the legislative spine for developing more effective and accessible services focused around the needs of children, young people and families.
   (www.everychildmatters.gov.uk/aims/background/)

The 'onion' diagram shown in Figure 3.1 is a visual representation of how services should be layered with a new emphasis on the integration of service approaches.

The emphasis on the sharing of information together with re-engineered processes and procedures to better support the needs of children was intended to be further strengthened by the co-location of services in children's centres and extended schools, using lead professionals and multidisciplinary teams.

   Every Child Matters: Change for Children programme aims to support parents from pregnancy onwards. The vision is to create a joined-up system of health, family support, childcare and education services so that all children get the best start possible in the vital early years.
   (http://publications.everychildmatters.gov.uk)

Every Child Matters sets out five key areas for children from birth to 19: being healthy; staying safe; enjoying and achieving; making a positive contribution; economic well-being. It provides for the establishment of Children's Trusts to organise ways and means to achieve success in these areas and has a clear intention of giving a real voice to children and young people. The emphasis is on local authorities to work with agencies through the Children's Trusts and to include children and young people as equal partners.

While there is cause for optimism in the underlying spirit there are fundamental difficulties in putting these new systems into place. While many areas are reorganising administration to reflect more joined-up approaches and potential partnerships, there is no single enforcing agency. It is difficult for change to be brought about when existing systems are designed for separate operations. Chapter 6 explores this aspect in more detail but essentially good will is not enough and cannot be relied on to be present, particularly in areas where the political sympathies are different from those of the government. In some ways the government have led by example and have consulted widely before shaping policy.

The Children's Plan

The Children's Plan of December 2007 was the result of consultation with children and young people, parents and experts in relevant fields. In his introduction the Secretary of State for Education, Ed Balls, emphasised the strengthening of support for families and their children from birth through the children's education and into the adult world. There are also emphases on involving parents in this process, creating safe places for young children to play and clear references to addressing the need for engaging children and young people outside school hours in 'interesting and exciting' activities. In the context of partnership working there is a clear statement of intent:

> The Plan and the new Department mean that more than ever before families will be at the centre of excellent, integrated services that put their needs first, regardless of traditional institutional and professional structures. This means a new leadership role for Children's Trusts in every area, a new role for schools as the centre of their communities, and more effective links between schools, the NHS and other children's services so that together they can engage parents and tackle all the barriers to the learning, health and happiness of every child.
>
> (Ed Balls, Secretary of State for Children, Schools and Families *The Children's Plan*, Foreword, pp. 1–2)

There are five underpinning principles:

- the need to support parents in bringing up their children;

- the recognition that children need to achieve their full potential;

- the assertion that children and young people should enjoy their childhood while preparing for adult life;

- the recognition that services should respond to needs rather than be limited by professional boundaries; and

- the recognition that preventing failure is better than addressing crises caused by it.

There is explicit recognition of changes in the demands the new system will make on leaders and professionals and therefore, by implication, for training and professional development. There is a clear statement on the need for leadership that is confident within the leader's own setting and in relationships between themselves and other leaders. In the Early Years specifically the emphasis is on leadership towards quality improvement, a positive learning culture and reflective practice aimed at improvement for staff as well as children (section 4.34, p. 89). This expectation of continuous improvement is intended to raise parents' understanding and expectation of quality care and education as well as to benefit the children.

While the emphasis on partnership working and the clear expectation of moving beyond traditional parameters and protocols are a boost to partnership working, the slightly concerning aspect from this perspective is the clear dominance of a single department, Education, in a document laying such emphasis on partnership working. Reference is made to working with NHS partners but it is disappointing that this is not a joint document. This unfortunate oversight reinforces the view that many involved in education hold that their perception is the most important and the one that counts when approaching the practical issues of partnership working. Although there is a strong emphasis on working with parents, it does little to support the open and equal approach to other partner agencies and professions where all views are valued which has been shown to work in examples in the preceding chapters. It seems to suggest that children's centres will be part of schools, which is potentially confusing for those already established separately. It also takes no account of the concerns raised in Chapter 6 regarding the fundamental differences between children's centres and schools and how these are to be overcome. There needs to be more explicit emphasis on the fact that schools and education professionals are included in the need to work towards new ways of working in partnership and away from traditional practices and constraints as part of the overall reform of public services (Anning et al., 2006: 127).

 Points for reflection

How will potential partners in Health, Social Services and Education view these aims?

What skills will be required by leaders of Early Years in light of the change of emphasis?

How can multi-agency working be built into training and development programmes?

What will be the role of parents, children and the local community?

The Early Years Foundation Stage

EYFS is the framework for settings to provide the educational quality referred to in and developed from: Curriculum Guidance for the Foundation Stage (DfEE/QCA, 2000); Birth to Three Matters (DfES, 2002) Framework and National Standards for Under 8s Daycare and Childminding (DfES, 2003). It sits alongside Every Child Matters and the Children's Plan. It is an attempt to combine the education and care agendas, as recommended by research such as the Effective Provision of Pre-School Education (EPPE) (DfES, 1997–2004) and the National Evaluation of Sure Start (NESS, 2005), to establish high-quality provision without imposing a prescriptive curriculum. It has the following key outcomes for children aged 0 to 8 years:

- A unique child

- Positive relationships

- Enabling environments

- Learning and development.

There is a strong emphasis on settings working in partnership with parents and other professionals to meet the needs of individual children and their families and on providing all-round, balanced opportunities for development and exploration. The EYFS recognises that children have different starting points and that development at the earliest stage is best achieved in partnership with families and carers, and emphasises the need to identify and meet additional learning needs as early as possible.

There was concern expressed by Edgington (2007) and others (e.g. Brighouse et al. 2007) that the Statutory Framework to the EYFS would be too prescriptive and restrict practice rather than allow freedom. However, the Statutory Framework documentation has been balanced by Practice Guidance which incorporates the underpinning principles and provides guidance on development and assessment which are based on established principles of Early Years education and care in England. These have become part of the EYFS standards known as the 'Key Elements of Effective Practice' (KEEP).

The KEEP that have been identified emphasise aspects of development which imply partnership working across professional boundaries. The KEEP provide more detail on the expectation set out in the Children's Plan for professionals to constantly improve by specifying improvement in:

- relationships with both children and adults;

- understanding of the individual and diverse ways that children learn and develop;

- knowledge and understanding in order to actively support and extend children's learning in and across all areas and aspects of Learning and Development;

- practice in meeting all children's needs, learning styles and interests;

- work with parents, carers and the wider community;

- work with other professionals within and beyond the setting.

(www.standards.dcsf.gov.uk/eyfs/site/about/index.htm)

The emphasis on developing and fostering relationships and balance between care aspects and education aspects, with the latter focusing on dispositions which underpin learning rather than specifying curriculum content, should encourage partnership working. There is an expectation of working together to support children's learning in its broadest sense. The expectation of professionals to increase their partnership working with parents and each other is clear.

In England the EYFS is directly linked to ECM which has more explicit guidance on the way partnership with all agencies involved with families should work. There are opportunities in the EYFS to do so, as indicated in the final bullet point above, but to succeed they will need the kind of creative partnerships advocated in ECM and the Children's Plan. The danger remains that the statements are open to a narrow interpretation creating an imbalance with undue educational emphasis and insufficient emphasis on child development, well-being and social care. Powell draws attention to areas in partnership working that need to be clarified and monitored if multi-agency working is to succeed:

- confusion about the legitimate role;

- lack of clarity about responsibilities and authority;

- disappointment that change was not fulfilling;

- conflicting priorities and working practices; and

- little systematic or effective sharing.

(Powell, in Nurse, 2007)

There will need to be specific attention given to these areas if ECM is to succeed in its partnership working dimensions. Anning et al. reinforce these aspects and expand the principles to be considered for successful partnership working (2006: 102ff.). Alongside these considerations, comments from practitioners emphasise the need for adequate funding and adequate time for negotiation, planning and reflection if initiatives involving partnership working are to succeed.

Without these factors effective and sustainable partnership working may not be achieved. In particular the vital perspectives provided through the specialist knowledge hold by practitioners from a Social Work or Health background over issues such as parenting and child development must not be restricted or lost. The link exists through ECM and the Children's Plan but challenging such deeply embedded professional cultures demands commitment, persistence and a sustained will to ensure lasting change takes place, with equal value and emphasis given to both ECM and the EYFS.

 Points for reflection

Where are the common themes and the differences between Every Child Matters, the Early Years Foundation Stage and the Children's Plan?

Where do multi-agency dimensions sit within and between these initiatives?

What has to change for these initiatives to achieve success?

The success of improvements in ECEC services in England is shown clearly in the Organisation for Economic Cooperation and Development report *Starting Strong* II

(OECD, 2006a: ch. 10). This was a major report commissioned by the OECD which looked in detail at ECEC provision in a comparative study covering 20 OECD member countries. It provides a comprehensive overview of contexts, focus and organisation of services available to children and families. The findings are particularly relevant in the context of this book because they illustrate the extent of integration of ECEC services, showing many of the subsequent benefits of integration in practice. The report notes significant improvement in the accessibility and quality of ECEC services in England between 2000 and 2006 and expresses the belief that services are on track to meet the espoused targets for 2010, although at the time of writing this does not now appear to the case for UK child poverty targets. Reservations are expressed over the significant shortfall in the workforce for ECEC and the persisting issues over economic constraints preventing access to ECEC services for low and lower-middle income families. The report acknowledges the potential for children's centres to meet a range of child and parental needs (OECD, 2006a: 415ff.). Interestingly the improvements and targets exceed most others included in the report and put the UK ahead in terms of partnership working. The continuing developments to support and extend ECEC services that are embedded in ECM, plus the developing Standards, the Early Years Quality Improvement Programme (EYQIP) and improvements to training at all levels, should help to maintain this progress.

Developments in Wales

The responsibility for ECEC services in Wales lies with the Welsh Assembly. In Wales, funding for Sure Start programmes has supported the development of area-based initiatives with a central 'hub' and outreach 'spokes' to enable local communities to access services which are partly offered and partly provided in response to consultation. Changes to improve partnership working began in April 2003 when a review and consultation led to the amalgamation of Sure Start in Wales with the Children and Youth Partnership Fund and the Childcare Strategy to form the Children and Youth Support Fund, known as Cymorth.

The six key aims reflect the UK government priorities in terms of:

- family support;

- health improvement;

- play, leisure and enrichment;

- empowerment, participation and active citizenship;

- training, mentoring and information; and

- building childcare provision.

The website includes information on integrated children's centres (ICCs) and lists 16 with interactive links. The ICCs are:

> ... based on the concept that providing integrated education, care, family support and health services is a key factor in determining good outcomes for children and their parents, ensuring the best start in life.
>
> (www.childreninwales.org.uk/inyourarea/ integchildcentres.html)

Figure 3.2   Sure Start Torfaen: the new building entrance. The building is in the grounds of a primary school and is readily accessible. The outdoor areas are being developed and building itself provides accommodation for a range of professional services.
Reproduced with permission from Torfaen.

The core provision for ICCs incorporates Early Years education, childcare, open access play, community education and training.

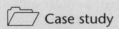 Case study

Torfaen ICC summary of reshaped provision

One local authority, Torfaen, provides a good example of the difference that has been made to the lives of families in areas where persisting high unemployment and low investment has created high social priority. Families where mothers have felt isolated and with low expectations have experienced new opportunities to meet together and learn new skills through the ICC. Self-esteem and confidence have increased. The services have developed from locations at the heart of communities, one in a converted block of flats scheduled for demolition and now shared with youth services and the local strategy group, another a St John's Ambulance Hall dating from 1938. Externally neither of these sites looks particularly promising yet the quality of work which goes on and the successes achieved is second to none and is helping to raise the expectations and ambitions of the young people and adults attending. Having shown what can be achieved the area has been provided with a brand new building of Scandinavian design to act as a 'hub' with the existing sites maintained as outreach 'spokes'. (see Figure 3.2 and 3.3). The new building shares part of a school grounds and is proving very successful in increasing the range and number of parents and children accessing services. The care and education agendas are complementary and are moving from co-location and cooperation to coordination.

Figure 3.3 Sure Start Torfaen: The doors give open access to the outdoor area. There are four large rooms at each corner, three used by the crèche, nursery and day care and one general purpose room use for parents groups, adult learning and activities.
Reproduced with permission from Torfaen.

Activity

Taking the example of the 'hub and spokes' model here, look at a map of your local area and plan your own children's centre.

Consider what professional and other agencies you would want to include.

What issues does this raise for creating partnerships?

What are the implications for parents and children accessing services?

To some extent the way ICC partnerships are organised and how they work in practice mirrors what has happened in England and has been encouraged and enabled by political initiatives and funding. It could be argued that the initial developments and the way in which parent and community consultation has been a significant part in shaping them have prepared the ground for more considered approaches to further development, drawing on contributions from researchers, politicians, practitioners, parents and communities.

Review in Wales has continued to move practice forward and to encourage more consistency and less rigidity. The implementation and outcomes of the pilot Welsh Foundation Stage were evaluated by Iram Siraj-Blatchford et al., who reported in 2008. This research found the highest quality pre-school provision in the public sector, with the private and voluntary sectors scoring more highly in areas of personal care. The best quality related directly to the numbers of trained teachers and was found in settings that used the Foundation Stage as guidance for practice rather than a rigid structure. While many staff in Reception and Year 1 welcomed the move towards learning through play, some found the change difficult and the report recommends a training programme to address this specific need. The report highlights differences in staff conditions between sectors which have a direct effect on the time available for planning. The report also raises questions about the kind of training needed to improve pedagogy, particularly for outdoor play and learning (which has supported the growing interest in Forest Schools), the need to address the variable provision in the private and voluntary sectors to avoid a two-tier system and how best to enhance practitioner and child interactions (Siraj-Blatchford et al., 2008).

Training, from Modern Apprenticeships in Care and Education for England and Wales to EYPS and degree level, will clearly need to be reviewed in the light of the report recommendations.

In terms of partnership working and the joined up agenda there still remains an apparent divide between the ICC and the Foundation Stage agendas. Many of the same issues affecting the relationship between children's centres and schools in England appear to be similarly affecting Wales, with the added issue in Wales of the significant gap between the private and voluntary and the state sectors. Specific and focused training will go part of the way to resolving the quality issue, but the need to find compatibility between Sure Start and school requires more: it requires a better understanding of the similarities and differences, the complementary and contradictory elements, at all levels from the strategic through the administrative all the way to the practitioners, in order to move towards more effective partnership.

Conclusions

This chapter has underscored what can be achieved when there is a combination of political will, adequate funding, consultative research, informed discussion and inclusive approaches where professionals, practitioners, children, parents and communities have an equal 'voice'. Where this happens new forms of practice can be developed which are relevant to needs and reflect cultural and social values, exemplified here by Forest Schools, Reggio Emilia and Te Whaariki. The political initiatives in England and Wales show how the climate for change can be encouraged and developed and how the vision can be set out and enabled. They emphasise the need to change the relationship between professionals and parents and children and professionals and each other. The example from Wales shows how services have been made available to parents and, in Chapter 2, how this has changed their lives.

This shows how the principles work from a local micro-level to the national and international macro-dimensions and at each stage in between.

What needs to be emphasised is the importance of recognising where each of those involved is starting from. The examples from other countries reflect their heritage and have been approached in ways that also reflect their cultural, social and political climates. The aims set out in England are being strengthened by additional structures such as EYQIP, regional forums for children's centre leaders and guidance for practitioners. Websites are providing information for parents who can access them. However, there also has to be the motivation and will, as well as the vision, for change to be effective. This has implications for leadership, explored in Chapter 6, and improved professional understanding, explored in Chapter 7.

The next chapter goes into more detail on the practical issues around partnership working.

 ## Summary

The key points to remember from this chapter are as follows:

- Partnership working in other countries has achieved significant improvement by combining shared philosophy, research, political will and funding, reflective practice and dialogue with children and parents.

- Examples from other countries underline the need for well planned, properly resourced partnership which is carefully implemented by well trained and well led professionals from all disciplines.

- Examples of innovative Early Years practice and organisation from other countries can provide new ideas and help us re-examine our own approaches.

- Increased partnership working is part of the foundation underpinning the government agenda for change and development in ECEC services in England but with DCFS and Education as the main agencies.

- The integrated children's centres in Wales have shown how successful partnership working achieves improvements for children and parents.

- Change in England and Wales will require improved quality of pre-school care and education, particularly in terms of strengthening the skill base of practitioners.

- In England and Wales in particular there is a lack of recognition or understanding of the key differences between the pre-school agenda, particularly as represented by Sure Start and children's centre agendas, and those of the school system, including extended schools.

- The real changes to the perception of the role of parents and changing practice as a result. The aim to include parents as equal partners was set out in the ten year strategy guidance for local authorities (DfES, 2005) and has been reinforced in succeeding legislation. Practice at local level has successfully embodied this change through Sure Start programmes and children's centres. However, there needs to be constant reinforcement if it is to become a lasting change.

Further reading 📖

For the report of findings in Wales:

- Siraj-Blatchford, I., Sylva, K., Laugharne, J., Milton, E. and Charles, F. (2006) *Monitoring and Evaluation of the Effective Implementation of the Foundation Phase (MEEIFP) Project Across Wales: Year 2 of Pilot.* Cardiff: Welsh Assembly Government.

In terms of policy making the following provides useful insights:

- Baldock, P., Fitzgerald, D., and Kay, J. (2009) *Understanding Early Years Policy* 2nd edn. London. Paul Chapman.

The following provides different international perspectives and discussions with implications for partnership working, including a closer look at the political roots of Reggio Emilia:

- Dahlberg, G., Moss, P. and Pence, A. (2007) *Beyond Quality in Early Childhood Education and Care: Postmodern Perspectives,* 2nd edn. London and New York: RoutledgeFalmer.

Specific reports referred to can be found at the following websites:

- Every Child Matters: www.everychildmatters.gov.uk/aims/background/

- The Children's Plan: www.dfes.gov.uk/publications/childrensplan/downloads/Childrens_Plan_ Executive_Summary.pdf

Useful websites

Forest Schools in England: www.forestschools.com

Reggio Emilia – the following provides a useful summary and includes additional reading

- www.communityplaythings.co.uk/resources/articles/reggio-emilia.html

Te Whaariki – the government website for New Zealand includes a detailed description of the Early Years curriculum including the underpinning cultural and philosophical aspects

- www.educate.ece.govt.nz/learning/curriculumAndLearning/TeWhaariki.aspx

Early Years Foundation Stage www.standards.dfes.gov.uk/eyfs/

Sure Start Children's Centres: www.togetherforchildren.co.uk; www.childrens-centres.org/ default.aspx

Sure Start Wales: www.surestart.gov.uk/aboutsurestart/help/contacts/wales/ www. early-years-nto.org.uk/keyskill_briefing_wales.pdf_

If you wish to find out more about other parts of the UK the following websites provide useful starting points:

- Information on the Growing Up in Scotland Study can be found at: www.scotland.gov.uk/ Publications/2007/01/17162004/2

- Information of Early Years including events, training, and conferences can be found at: www. ltscotland.org.uk/earlyyears/sharingpractice/index.asp

- Sure Start Scotland: www.surestart.gov.uk/aboutsurestart/help/contacts/scotland/

- Sure Start Northern Ireland: www.surestart.gov.uk/aboutsurestart/help/contacts/northernireland/

Partnership working in practice

Chapter 1 introduced the idea of partnership working, Chapter 2 provided an overview of aims and practice and Chapter 3 looked at case studies from other countries and developments in England and Wales. This chapter looks more closely at examples from practice to show more detail of the organisation of partnership working and children's centres and its effects, including:

- different models of multi-agency organisation;
- how different settings respond to the needs of their communities;
- the range of stakeholders;
- case study examples of services provided;
- leadership and management issues.

Context

Joint approaches to issues affecting children and families are not new and different kinds of cooperation have existed for some time. For example, medical services and social services have worked in varying degrees of partnership with schools, and if you include the welfare of child patients hospitals also work with other social care agencies. In these examples there is a clearly defined 'lead' agency and the other services tend to physically come to the lead agency premises. Perhaps the most well-known example is when Social Services hold case conferences around child protection issues, when there will be representatives from all parties involved in a case, which may include education, health visitors, GPs, police, foster parents and community mental health, and can include support for the parent(s). In most cases these are case-specific and short-term partnerships, essentially after an event or concern has been lodged. The kind of partnership envisaged now and for the future is longer term and is essentially intended to be proactive rather than reactive at a stage before a serious referral needs to be made. In approaching an understanding of how this can work several of the works referred to in this book provide examples from across former boundaries. For example, Anning et al. (2006) present a study of five teams with partnerships across health, police, probation service, voluntary sector, social services/city council and education, Barnett et al. (2005) focus on a health and social care perspective, while Weinstein et al. (2003) focus on social practice and Barr et al. (2005) are based in health. An essential aspect is that children and young people, parents and communities are seen as equal partners with an important 'voice': that the partnership will be seen as 'working with' rather than 'doing to', a subtle but important distinction that alters the fundamental dynamic of the relationship. What is required is a clearer knowledge and understanding of good practice within and between teams which link across professional spheres and their common factors.

In establishing children's centres the government drew on existing experience from Sure Start and Early Excellence Centres. While responsibility was devolved to local authorities, there was existing good practice to draw on in terms of the overall organisation and reach of settings and groups and their internal organisation. So how does this work in practice? The following sections use examples from practice to illustrate different themes and approaches.

Organisation

While the external organisation is down to local authorities to whom centres are accountable, internal organisation is down to individual centres but with an expectation that a 'partnership board' (sometimes referred to as a steering group or steering committee) will have oversight of the direction and development of services. This board is meant to represent all 'stakeholders' within the centre reach area and must include parents. The example below shows the potential for positive outcomes but also how difficult it can be when individual partners have a fixed idea centred around their own perspective.

Collaborative partnership boards

The best example is the collaborative partnership board, now developed into the advisory board. When the partnership works well together then services are much more joined up. However, in the early days of the Sure Start Local Programme (SSLP), there were partners who came to the table with additional motives to obtain capital funding or revenue funding within their own organisations. This led to conflict between partners when jostling for funds. At one time a board member was asked to resign as they were in danger of bringing the partnership board into disrepute.

Many multi-agency settings developed from Sure Start Local Programmes. These programmes had partnership boards with representation from a wide range of stakeholders. Parents were encouraged to take an active part but this was not easy to establish. Many parents either lacked confidence or else saw this as an opportunity for specific personal issues to be pursued. Professional partners also came to the table with their own agendas and experiences too. They were used to committees, were more familiar with procedures and were skilled in using formal meetings to achieve their own needs. The notion of more open meetings with a genuine sharing and open exchange of views was something that centre leaders had to establish. Centre leaders had a difficult task to find the right balance yet maintain a positive input from all, including parents. Parents finding themselves in the centre of such conflicts can feel isolated and find it hard to contribute. In many cases the language, acronyms and jargon used can prevent clear understanding and emphasise the 'exclusivity' of those who understand. Centre leaders had to find new ways to structure meetings and to break down the barriers to communication. An example of innovative committee practice has been the exploration of values, aims and principles undertaken collectively in a workshop style. This kind of activity has been reinforced by the National Professional Qualification in Integrated Centre Leadership (NPQICL) which encourages creative and experiential approaches. In such situations all are truly equal, can contribute equally and at the end achieve a shared understanding of why they are there. At the same time the nature of the process helps to break down barriers and encourages individuals to get to know other team members. Where this works advisory boards and management groups can achieve positive outcomes for the centre, as the next example shows.

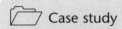 Case study

Successful partnership organisation

[This] has been one of the [best] children's centres I have been involved with: the site consisted of an education nursery which also incorporated a family centre team. The education aspect focused on the 3–5 education elements while the family centre team focused on targeted support to children under 5. The centre became an Early Excellence Centre in 1999 and in 2002 combined its capital funding with the local Sure Start programme to improve the facilities on offer. This allowed for the development of a day nursery for children 0–5, a base for the Sure Start team, additional office space for the family centre team and the development of a large community room.

This enabled each team to join together to offer a holistic approach to families that put the child's needs at the centre of provision. A multi-agency team consisting of managers from education, day care, the family centre team and Sure Start meets weekly to consider the logistics of the centre and decide day-to-day management issues. The board of governors while not having overall responsibility for the Sure Start Children's Centre services, the day care or the family team, considers reports from these groups, and managers from these areas including education sit on this group. The benefits of this joined up approach have been:

- greater involvement by the community in the centre as all staff have adopted a community empowerment mode of practice;
- non-stigmatised services because staff work across areas so any member of staff from any team may be working with particular children;
- a more joined-up approach to meeting the needs of children – children who may need more intensive support than the school can offer access day care provision which has lower ratios;
- staff gain experience of working in other areas and are therefore more able to deal with the children they are working with;
- the needs of the child come first and who is best able to deliver that service will do so;
- because of a multi-agency approach services are not just delivered in term time only – Sure Start may have provided some funding but it has been education workers who have delivered the services – so children have the advantage of being in an environment they know with staffing they know;
- service level agreements have helped to structure what services are to be commissioned and what needs to be achieved by local organisations for the delivery of provision which meets the core offer.

The above example shows clearly the benefits to be gained from a commitment to combining resources for the benefit of children, families and communities. Having a shared vision and clear focus on the centrality of the needs of the children and also on increasing community involvement meant greater and more meaningful contact. Combining financial resources in this case provided additional physical space, additional staff with specific skills and additional services relevant to the needs of children, families and communities. The setting up of a joint multi-agency team committed to shared aims meant that needs could be regularly assessed and reviewed and staff allocated appropriately according to need. Staff shared the leaderhsip vision and were prepared to work creatively, unrestricted by more conventional roles. The governing body was able to provide a forum for debate and discussion and establish strategies that all members contributed to. In addition, service level agreements (SLAs), that is where services are provided by one agency for another under agreed contractual terms and usually at a specified financial rate, allowed the combination of funding from one source and staffing from another to enable continuous provision of a service throughout the year. Creative funding and arrangements of this kind can be the key difference in creating or maintaining a service but they can be difficult to achieve and require trust and understanding on the part of board members. In this case the agreement transformed services and enabled an approach which could not otherwise have been achieved. (SLAs are discussed more fully below.)

The listed benefits show direct improvement for the children, families and communities through better access to a wider range of services appropriate to their needs. The benefits to staff are based on the premise that they themselves are able and willing to take on flexible working to support children and families, working as a team with shared vision and aims, which requires careful leadership and training. The case study provides insights into the ethos of partnership working and the way in which new approaches to organisation can create a climate which enables new forms of partnership to be conceived and developed. How these work is explored further below.

Service level agreements

Service level agreements have helped to structure what services are to be commissioned by settings themselves and in partnerships between agencies. They set out what needs to be achieved by local organisations for the delivery of provision which meets the core offer generally and specific services in particular. Designing service level agreements requires negotiation skills and knowledge of what is possible for partner agencies to agree. A key aspect of partnership working is to open discussion in order to explore the constraints and find new ways of achieving what is needed, yet stay within acceptable fiscal and organisational parameters. Once established the agreements are not inflexible but require monitoring so that necessary adjustments can be proposed and discussed.

Such agreements are key to ensuring a service is able to achieve the intended provision and to identifying parameters which define the role and expectation of staff delivering the service. This may involve centre staff themselves or external staff or combinations of both. The details of staff accountability and support mechanisms are equally important to establish and clarify. Commissioned services will mean the

Figure 4.1   Dad and child at a children's centre in the North West
Reproduced with permission.

staff are employed by an agency outside the centre with an external line manager, yet be responsible in role to the centre leader as their line manager on site. Successful working depends on the quality of understanding between the external provider leaders involved and the staff and centre leader and colleagues. In most cases the commissioned staff will be treated as full members of staff while in their role. This demands particular attitudes from core staff based in the centre and those from other agencies working on site and requires a willingness to be flexible and accommodating from everyone. This places new demands on everyone involved including service and centre leaders.

 Points for reflection

Think about the issues of mutual respect.

What is the value of respect in building working relationships?

Does partnership working work well within your centre, and do you all have a good working relationship and respect each other's heritage?

Many settings work closely with fathers and have established good relationships. Figures 4.1 and 4.2 show dads with their children at a centre in the North West. The pictures speak for themselves in terms of bonding, trust and sheer pleasure.

Challenges

Another key to success is the mutual respect and respect for the professional backgrounds and individual viewpoints which underpin the quality of relationships

Figure 4.2   Fathers and toddlers at a children's centre in the North West
Reproduced with permission.

between staff based at each centre and those with whom they work in partnership. It is not possible for staff to contain themselves within their own sphere of work or 'silo'. All staff need to understand the whole picture and how each part depends on the others to maintain overall cohesion and consistency in addition to being competent in their own area. Sharing information at all levels is essential, even when this means working around protocols concerned with communication which may differ between partner agencies and different professional backgrounds. A common stumbling block has been around interpretations of the Data Protection Act 1998. Some agencies or individuals within them believe the Act means that no information can be passed on, exchanged or even referred to outside that agency. So an Act designed to protect individuals becomes a barrier to communication that would enable closer partnership built on deeper understanding that would permit the needs of those individuals to be better and more efficiently met. However, some individuals and agencies have managed to work within the spirit of the Act rather than a narrow interpretation of the letter, by finding ways of acknowledging that information may exist without disclosing details.

 Case study

Meeting the challenge of conflicting principles and rules: making data protection work without infringing the protection of individual's personal information

A partnership team involving a school, social services and health visitors was able to work within the spirit of data protection by simply acknowledging to each other that *there was an issue* without identifying the details. In this way the school, social services and health, who all had different concerns about a child's family situation, were able to avoid taking separate action that would have worked against each other and the family, because they were alerted to the fact that each had an involvement. Sharing this basic information meant that isolated decision-making was avoided and a more helpful joint strategy could be developed. The family was supported and enabled to move forward, rather than feel victimised by inappropriate, although procedurally correct, actions.

 Points for reflection

What difference does professional background make?

What attitudes and approaches will those involved need to have for successful partnership working?

How can the requirement to keep to procedures and rules be balanced with the obligation to identify and meet the specific needs of children, families and communities?

Partnerships and children's centres are pioneers of new ways of working and have to meet challenges presented by legal and procedural constraints as well as those that are simply 'common practice' or assumed to be universal when in reality they are part of the way of working for one agency only. This predisposition of agencies and professions to certain attitudes and interpretations is referred to as 'professional heritage'. This colours the perspective each brings and can be both a positive and a negative force: positive in that it enriches debate and brings new insights; negative in that individuals may only see one view point which they believe is 'right' and be reluctant to change this perspective as a result. Particularly difficult situations can occur when the same word has a subtly or completely different meaning in two or more professions. For example, 'supervision' is a positive and fulfilling experience in Social Services and Health but in Education tends to have a negative or even disciplinary connotation suggesting that an individual is not yet able to manage on their own. Assumptions that all understand what is being said or proposed in the same way can cause misunderstandings. The following example illustrates the frustration that can occur between agencies that are assumed to be similar but which are fundamentally different in philosophy, ethos and practice, specifically schools and children's centres.

Care and Education: different perspectives

As a children's centre, we have had many difficulties working with our local schools and in particular the provision of a teacher which is a requirement. There are tensions because of different expectations about the role of a children's centre teacher and there are different interpretations between the setting and the schools. It is known that the setting is a development area and one where there will be difficulties until all can see the way forward.

On the positive side there are very good links with Homestart where there is trust and a common ambition to support families.

This opens a really critical area which is explored in more depth in Chapter 5. There is an assumption on the part of many local authorities and others that schools and children's centres are essentially the same: they both deal with very young children and families; they are located in specific areas to serve the needs of the community; and the extended schools agenda is essentially the same as the children's centre agenda. Unfortunately these assumptions are not correct. Schools are essentially the beginning of the formal education system. While many schools may well have a progressive view of how best to achieve the national aims and standards, many are still very formal in their approach. Children's centres emphasise *care* and education while schools emphasise *education* and care – a subtle but important difference which is emphasised internally by the different ethos of the Foundation Stage compared with later stages in education. Children's centres are essentially child and family centred and serve several schools, even though many are sited on one specific school site.

Unfortunately the lack of understanding of the importance of this last key point has meant that some local authorities have simply taken advantage of spare capacity to adapt rooms to create children's centres within schools or have extended school buildings or provided new buildings alongside schools, irrespective of the difference in ethos, aims, attitudes and atmosphere. This is not to say that partnership working between children's centres and schools cannot succeed. It may well be that as Early Childhood Care and Education services develop in future, more open and flexible approaches will become the accepted norm and enable more open, less distancing structures. If this is so it has yet to be shared or discussed with many schools, their governors or headteachers. To achieve success there has to be a greater understanding of the differences and the starting points and greater support and training for all those involved.

The place of teachers in children's centres illustrates the dilemma between power and authority. The example above illustrates how difficult it can be for a trained teacher to adapt to the ethos and approaches which reflect the more open philosophy of children's centres. This has not been helped by the initial compromise which led to the requirement that all children's centres must have 0.5 of a teacher in each setting. Some providers approached this by allocating a qualified teacher to oversee several children's centres. In other cases those appointed found themselves overseeing and accountable for practice and were rapidly promoted, even though they had little experience or knowledge of children's centres or partnership working. In very many cases the assumptions over the superior qualification, knowledge, power and authority of teachers combined with higher salaries created additional issues which are still not resolved, although many centre leaders have found ways to minimise the more negative effects and develop the positives.

How the role of teacher within children's centres will develop is open to conjecture. The pathways to qualification as a teacher have become more diverse and more accessible, but the way teachers and teaching assistants work in schools has changed a great deal, with teachers in more strategic and supervisory roles. This is even truer of the role of teachers within children's centres. The emergence of the Early Years Professional Status to provide professionals trained to work across health, care and education could provide a way forward but will depend on the quality of the training and on whether it is seen as a cheap or easy option to local authorities and organisations. (This is explored more fully in Chapter 7.) A perceived 'blurring of the distinction between a teacher and an EYP [Early Years Professional] raises the possibility of a distinct (and perhaps lower paid/lower status) category of teachers trained for pre-school settings' (Anning and Ball, 2008: 8). How successful the deployment of EYPs to all children's centres by 2010 may be will not only depend on the quality of training and how the qualification is perceived by the profession, but also on the ability of the individual to be flexible and at home with approaches that are open, accommodating, and non-judgemental. This cannot be assumed and may be difficult for those embedded within a different professional culture and heritage.

Specific services

The detailed list of responses from children's centre leaders given in Table 4.1 indicates the wide range of services and points of contact which are masked by the general headings used to describe the core services. The services listed also hint at the innovative and entrepreneurial ways in which centres have approached the provision of services through partnerships with other providers, acting as facilitators and providing premises for the specific services listed. Many medical and health services, such as

Table 4.1   Results of survey*

No of times mentioned	Service
12	Health visitors Head teachers and school staff/education
9	Midwives Adult education staff/Learning Skills Council Job Centre Plus Social workers/social care
8	Local voluntary organisations (Bangladeshi Women Resource Centre) Health/PCT (Primary Care Trust) Speech and language therapists
7	FE college staff Advisory staff including Special Educational Needs (SEN) (Hearing and Visually Impaired), extended schools coordinator, pupil referral units (PRUs) Homestart
6	Education psychologists/psychologists
5	Community forum/community leaders/voluntary community groups/Safer Neighbourhood Group Physiotherapists Sexions (sexual health for young people) National Consortium of Colleges (NCC) Development worker Library/senior library officer Play development Community care
4	Other Early Years settings University staff/university Other voluntary organisations/pre-school Learning Alliance (PSLA) School nurse/health visitor Community pediatricians Connexions Family support/befrienders Welfare rights Hettys

(Continued)

Table 4.1   (Continued)

No of times mentioned	Service
3	GPs
	Faith groups – local churches
	Housing/housing association
	Family centres
	Children's and young people's team,
	Domestic abuse team
	Councils (town/borough/county/district)
2	Nursery
	Extended schools
	Faith groups – local mosques
	Citizens' Advice Bureau (CAB)
	Occupational therapists
	Portage staff
	Family resource team staff/family learning
	Childminders/child care providers
	Community and Adolescent Mental Health Services (CAMHs)
	Dentist
	Local police/fire
	Local agencies (Early Years)
	Community development officer/youth service
1	Chair of governors (school)
	Out-of-school clubs
	Kid West Midlands
	Local Somali charities
	My training provider
	Nutritionist
	Local education officers
	Local Safeguarding Board
	National Childbirth Trust (NCT)
	Inclusion teams
	Family information service
	Parents
	Extended schools workers/extended schools
	Coral Health
	Relate
	Family Link Project
	Music project
	Active Sports
	BAPS (Breastfeeding and Peer Support)
	Parents with prospects
	Young mums to be
	Forest School
	Private organisations (Tumble Tots)
	Play development
	Neighbourhood centre staff
	STAR (Supporting Tenants and Residents)
	Children's Information Service
	CAF coordinator
	Mothers and Learners Together (MALT)
	Inclusion support
	Parish councils
	Women's Aid
	Integrated services
	Children's Trust

*The responses in this table are from 23 children's centre heads across a range of types (stand-alone, school site, more than one site) and local authorities, representing a 12 per cent return from the 190 children's centre leaders surveyed for this research. The numbers refer to the frequency with which the services concerned were mentioned.

Figure 4.3 Parents and babies attend swimming run by a children's centre in the North West
Reproduced with permission.

midwifery, health visitors and speech and language therapy, use staff employed
directly or indirectly by the centre. The range and number of these services seems to
suggest they represent the greatest volume from a specific profession and reflect the
diversity of services covered by one profession and the emphasis on health nationally. In addition to the listed services, anecdotal evidence seems to suggest that there
is a greater willingness for some specialists, for example psychologists, to donate additional clinic time and one to one sessions beyond their contracted commitment. The
more 'blanket' coverage provided by core services is evident, with Education and
Social Services featuring significantly alongside Health, but the table also illustrates
the wide range of locally framed services which shows clearly how settings have
responded to local needs in areas such as counselling and domestic violence support,
baby massage, respite care support, work with fathers and financial management. The
frequency of examples referred to once or twice represents about half the total list.

Many centres facilitate sessions requested by parents by commissioning them
through other providers or by using their own staff, and sessions may be on or off
site as Figure 4.3 shows.

 Points for reflection

What are the implications for practitioners and leaders of providing such a
potentially wide range of services?

What kind of skills will practitioners and leaders need to identify, set up and run
services which match the core offer?

How can parents *not* be included as equal partners?

Each of the agencies involved in partnership working and each of the individuals employed at centres will have specific training and experience in a specialist area. We all are influenced by the heritage of our own working background. Before we can begin to fully work in partnership we each have to recognise our own predispositions and preferred ways of working and thinking about work. Once we acknowledge this and begin to understand how we approach issues, we can begin to see the potential benefits provided by differing professional perspectives as well as understanding the challenges.

Children's centres are developing their own professional heritage characterised by openness, accessibility, flexibility, listening, reflection and negotiation. Their approach to partnership working aims to be more open to suggestions and less focused on single approaches to specific ends. Centre leaders aim to encourage dialogue to find new ways through potential barriers, recognising the value in the different perspectives and skills which partners bring to the discussion. Initial meetings are often characterised by members generally starting from very particular attitudes and assumptions which have been important and fundamental to the independent success of their profession while working in a distinct area. Creating an atmosphere where individuals have the desire to work together with a vision of greater possibilities is a key part of the roles of all staff at all levels in children's centres. However, dependence on individuals can only be a short-term strategy because individuals move on. Longer-term success requires changes to fundamental attitudes and relationships at an agency or professional level. This is explored in more depth in Chapters 5 and 6.

An important step is to get away from the view that partnership working means others join in the partnership based on the terms and assumptions of one profession or agency (a 'they work with us' model). Developing the sharing of understanding, values and aims helps to create a willingness to work towards a shared goal (a 'we work together' model). Planning and preparation is essential if longer-term success is to be achieved. Regular review with an open and depersonalised critical approach allows refinements and adjustments to be made that will further strengthen the service and the partnership.

 Points for reflection

What attitudes and approaches will encourage parents who were disillusioned at school and professionals who are embedded within their own professional culture to feel welcomed and valued within a children's centre or partnership team?

What will put them off?

The following case study provided by a children's centre leader explores some of the issues around their experience of partnership working, including those that arise from differences in structural as well as professional or cultural predispositions.

 Case study

One children's centre experience of partnership working with the Citizens Advice Bureau service

We identified a need for benefits, debt and immigration advice so forged a partnership with the CAB via a service level agreement. It was clear from the shared data from this partnership, about confirmed and estimated monetary gains, that the families were benefiting a lot.

The area also suffers from high unemployment but we did hear some success stories about active children's centre volunteers who gained part-time employment without affecting their benefits and of others who made the effort to explore getting jobs.

One flaw in the partnership was that the CAB organisation's policy needed to be respected in terms of having no service for two weeks around Christmas but council policy stated that a service should be provided during all council core working hours. Another flaw was that the post was part-time therefore when the CAB worker was off sick or absent or training, the service suffered unless another worker was sent, but more often than not this was not possible.

One of the lessons learnt through the arrangement with the CAB is that often partner agencies attach huge management costs and hidden costs which create tensions for the children's centre organisation. This is especially so when profiling budgets during times of budget cuts. On these occasions the costly partnerships would be the first to go in order to retain the children's centre's core services.

This example highlights some of the realities of partnership working. Outside agencies cannot separate one element from their whole profile. Unless the provision of a service working with a children's centre is seen somehow as essential and part of the core, it is likely to be the first casualty if finances become stretched or protocols are challenged. Maintaining continuity can be very difficult, particularly when the individual providing the service has worked to establish relationships with service users and staff at the centre. Another issue can be the monitoring of the quality of service provided, and how to deal with aspects that are unsatisfactory or not in keeping with the centre ethos, particularly when the centre manager does not oversee the individual concerned. However, as the next case study shows, issues can be successfully resolved if the partnership works creatively.

 Case study

An example of good practice of partnership working between Sure Start Children's Centres and Jobcentre Plus

The opening challenge for the year was that Jobcentre Plus had rung to say they were cancelling their sessions due to staff shortages and poor uptake of their service in the centre. This was a heart-sinking moment for the centre staff as a positive relationship had developed between both partners over the previous year. A telephone call to the local office revealed a familiar story of pressure around agency targets. Managers were juggling with competing needs and staff shortages. A follow-up call to the childcare partnership manager (CPM) highlighted a recurring theme nationally. She was, however, eager to meet with the centre coordinator to re-establish links.

At this meeting the CPM and the coordinator explained their roles to each other around the targets and activities of the five Every Child Matters outcomes and core offer. The type of engagement between parents and advisors was discussed which focused especially on how the advisors felt about our requests for more active engagement in terms of joining in activities with

(Continued)

parents and staff. An issue highlighted was that the advisors reported a lack of confidence and experience of being in such close contact with customers and other agencies in informal settings and that support was needed.

As a result of the issues raised at this meeting and further discussions within the team it was felt that a positive step in the engagement process would be to invite a member of Jobcentre Plus to the district team development day. The outcome was a constructive step towards a stronger partnership. The advisor who attended suggested ways forward, reporting that she had reflected upon what she had learned from the day in terms of the Sure Start vision and felt she had a part to play. The outcome for families has been a service that attends regularly on set days in the month and a service that is more focused on their needs. For example, there are now opportunities not only to offer general advice but also to offer focused activities such as completing work-focused interviews and taking referrals for benefit and tax credit advice.

This example illustrates the importance of children's centre leaders and senior staff taking the initiative and actively seeking dialogue with partners, but also being sensitive to partner needs and providing support where required. If the decision had simply been accepted without question or discussion the service would have ceased to be offered. All staff need to be constantly aware and need to review continuously how services are working or may need to be adjusted. Dialogue is critical to improving understanding and leaders must be prepared to open discussion rather than wait or expect someone else to do so. The benefits are further explored in the next example described by a children's centre leader.

 Case study

An illustration of the value to be gained from proactive practice in partnership working

The setting staff were very aware that there was a range of holiday services being provided across the area by combinations of private providers, the district council, voluntary groups, the youth service and children's centre.

It was decided to form a task and finish group to look at existing provision and identify the gaps. The group which represented the range of providers was formed and led by the Community and Learning Partnership (C&LP) Coordinator (line managed by the centre leader). The group identified what was needed – additional funding was provided by the C&LP to enable additional activities. It was decided that some of the activities would be jointly delivered by the youth service and district council. Some services would have a cost, but targeted groups would be supported. This was linked to community transport to provide a collection service from rural areas and those families who have been referred by other professionals. The district council already produced a parents' information leaflet to advertise the services provided so it was decided that the contents of this would be expanded to contain details of the other activities provided by the private and voluntary sector/ youth service/children's centre. In this way a choice was provided for parents and children.

An audit of the all the services is now available. It is to be put on plasma screens in schools/children's centre/leisure centre. Hopefully there will now be an improved service across the area which has cost a minimum amount of funding due to the partnership working.

The responsibility for starting the process of dialogue lay with the centre leader. As a result of their initial action, a multi-agency group was brought together and then took ownership of the process and subsequent shared actions. The funding could have been an issue but was overcome by not being constrained by a single formula or process. Instead a range of approaches was used and funding came from different partners. Rather than a limiting and divisive 'what's in it for us?' approach, this positive 'what can we provide?' approach achieved far more. The success of this partnership depended on generating goodwill and recognising and valuing the potential contribution of each of the partners, irrespective of status or sector.

The example might seem to be too good to be true but there were issues that arose:

- waiting for the information to be returned from all the partners;

- fear from private and voluntary agencies that they would be squeezed out of service provision;

- permission from some managers was slow in being given;

- developing referral criteria and communicating this to other professionals.

These issues are common to many new partnerships. The coordinating partner has a specific sense of priority which may not be matched by other partners outside the meeting. It is also very common for fear to be a major initial factor among partners developing their opening trust and both these aspects require understanding, patience, reassurance and tact to overcome. The final issue reflects the different practices and approaches adopted by partner agencies. Agreeing procedures means beginning to create understanding that there are different approaches which are based on differing priorities and philosophies, which may not have occurred to some of the partners. Communicating decisions also needs care and tact as those who were not present will have no background or contextual knowledge of how decisions were made and may not appreciate actions or procedures that suddenly appear. In this example the setting was able to overcome these issues and succeed in their aim of coordinating a multi-agency group, enabling them to work with, rather than against, each other. The networking between providers also had the potential to enable families, children and communities to see more clearly what was available and to have better access.

Chapter 5 explores the importance of wide consultation in assessing needs. Knowing what to provide is a beginning: knowing how to establish it and set it in motion requires careful planning. Being creative in approaching the introduction and setting up of new services can mean that a result can be achieved by a less direct route, including how staff will be employed and funded. Lateral thinking can help to overcome issues that cannot be addressed by existing approaches, but this is complex and not always initially successful.

Arrangements where premises are owned by one body and staff using the site are paid by another are becoming more common but still require careful planning and consultation within partnerships to establish and maintain. This is simple enough to set out on paper but involves complex organisation, including the establishing of areas of joint and separate responsibilities, line management issues, and funding and accountability pathways. Being well intentioned is not enough and it is important to anticipate likely consequences.

The next example shows what can happen when a good intention is not thought through and agencies insist on conditions which make sense within their own practice but which do not match the needs of the partnership.

> Commonly, workers from one children's centre area are seconded to another agency in a nearby area within the same town. This has the benefit of staff being able to share practice knowledge and develop a network of contacts with other professionals. However, there can be constraints and drawbacks, for example where line management arrangements are not fully discussed which leads to failures in HR practice and disadvantages to individual staff, or where further insistence that seconded staff may work only within the prescribed boundaries of the host agency leads to frustrations from the original agency. In one case this became particularly acute when the children's centre received a priority referral from a health visitor to support the transition into nursery of one family's three-year-old child. The host agency insisted upon maintaining strict boundaries which worked directly to the disadvantage of the family and the child was not able to be supported to make a prompt transition into the nursery. The family was left feeling confused, the child did not have prompt and successful access into a much needed nursery place, and relations between agencies were negative.

The above shows some of the aspects that need more careful planning and groundwork before real success can be achieved. Reflecting on the positives and negatives will help settings to move towards greater success. The host agency described above was only willing to go part of the way towards meeting the needs of this partnership. Partial commitment may be a step in the right direction but if it is likely to act against the overall aims, it is better left for further negotiation. Where issues arise for individual agencies it may be difficult for them to revisit internal procedures and rules, particularly if this appears to be creating inconsistent practice, but this may be necessary in exceptional cases. The example below shows how partial awareness and partial willingness is not enough and that recognising what will and will not work is essential.

Many of the issues identified in this chapter are addressed in an Australian study conducted by Paul Aylward, at the University of Adelaide, and Margaret O'Neil, Lady Gowrie Theobarton, Adelaide, in the 'Through the Looking Glass' project (2009) at the University of Adelaide. The project involved health, social workers and early childhood care and education staff working together. Aylward and O'Neil describe how relationships and behaviours within separate professional groups were strong but worked against the full partnership. The report supports similar findings in England:

- a preference to consult with colleagues from the same discipline;

- a privileging of sharing information and resources within the same discipline as colleagues (at the expense of interdisciplinary co-workers who became excluded from much professional dialogue);

- an over-theorising about parent issues – the emergence/strengthening of professional jargon that was less accessible to the early childhood professionals;

- a sense of professional and intellectual competitiveness;

- the witholding of information in relation to clients from early childhood professionals justified by 'confidentiality';

- a demand from the health team that they required separate and 'more complex' professional development opportunities;

- a (worrying) sense from the health team that their intervention was of greatest significance.

It was clear that the traditional professional hierarchy put care workers at the lowest point regardless of qualification. Members of the childcare team also became anxious about working in partnership. To solve these issues settings partly re-recruited when some members left, but also ensured the newly formed group had a clearer idea of the aims and intentions and, critically, the line management structures. Joint planning helped as did also a careful restructuring of the initial assessment where the child's care worker was observed with the parent and child and therefore became much more involved in the initial assessment process. A participant noted:

> Providing cultural symbols for project staff to identify with has been helpful – joint celebrations of achievements, combined conference papers and presentations, all of the public representations of the project are important for building a symbolic representation of a united team.

The report's conclusions provide clear guidance on key areas for developing Early Years partnership networks, including:

- the need to promote change through continuous improvement;

- the value of establishing a culture of reflection and evaluation; the importance of a shared vision;

- the gains from strategic networking;

- the benefits of creating teams that are truly multi-disciplinary and services which are fully integrated;

- the need for staff to have access to continuing professional development; and

- the value of creativity and innovation.

Aylward and O'Neil's findings support those in Chapter 6 and Chapter 7 in terms of the characteristics of those involved in partnership working and the factors that positively enable successful partnership working. These show the prime aims of partnership working and the key areas which need to be addressed for it to succeed. These prime aims include:

- identifying and responding to the needs of children, families and the wider community;

- taking account of the needs of the whole family;

- being adaptable and flexible in approaches;

- bringing services to the community rather than the reverse;

- improving accessibility;

- developing open dialogue with agencies as the foundation of partnership working.

Summary

The key points to remember from this chapter are:

- Partner agencies need to have clear aims, principles and values and be prepared to apply these to their own working.
- Effective partnership involves children, families and communities as equal partners.
- There need to be clear definitions of working relationships, roles, parameters, protocols, responsibility and accountability.
- Good communication between all involved is essential to success.
- There needs to be understanding of what each of the partners brings and respect for each other's points of view and perspectives.
- There needs to be willingness to listen and willingness to be creative and flexible.
- There is sometimes a clash between service needs as perceived by agencies and those desired by communities: identifying needs and designing services to match has to include the views of children, families and communities.
- Awareness of the need to constantly review and adjust is essential.

Further reading

Themes around partnership working are explored in:

- Anning, A., Cottrell, D., Frost, N., Green, J. and Robinson, R. (2006) *Developing Multiprofessional Teamwork for Integrated Children's Services: Research, Policy and Practice.* Maidenhead: McGraw Hill Education/Open University Press.

Specifically focused on improving children's life chances and well worth reading is:

- Gardner, R. (2003) 'Working together to improve children's life chances: the challenge of inter-agency collaboration', in J. Weinstein, C. Whittington and T. Leiba (eds), *Collaboration in Social Practice*. London: Jessica Kingsley, pp. 137–60.

With reference to social workers (Rummery) and the care of the elderly (Lymbrey), the principles raised by each in terms of partnership working are comparable. For more detail see:

- Rummery, K. (2003) 'Social work and multi-disciplinary collaboration in primary health care', in J. Weinstein, C. Whittington and T. Leiba (eds), *Collaboration in Social Practice*. London: Jessica Kingsley, pp. 201–17, pp. 214ff.

- Lymbrey, M. (2003) 'Collaborating for the social and health care of older people', in J. Weinstein, C. Whittington and T. Leiba (eds), *Collaboration in Social Practice*. London: Jessica Kingsley, pp. 219–38, pp. 221ff.

To read more about multi-agency working see:

- Colmer, K. (2008) 'Leading a learning organization: Australian early years centres as learning networks', *European Early Childhood Education Research Journal*, 16 (1): 107–15.

A summary of extended services covering both schools and children's centres is provided in:

- Ofsted (2006) *Extended Services in Schools and Children's Centres*, HMI 2609.

Useful websites

For Every Child Matters go to: http://www.everychildmatters.gov.uk/aims/background/

More examples from practice can be found at:

- www.childrens-centres.org/Topics/FAQ/CCFAQ.aspx

- www.childrens-centres.org/default.aspx

5

Why partnership working matters

This chapter looks closely at how to identify the needs of children and therefore best address those needs as part of the team as well as offering examples of key success stories from practice which illustrate the:

- benefits for children and families;
- benefits for professionals;
- benefits for local communities.

Key terms

In this chapter the following terms are used with these definitions:

The role of parents – refers to the *potential* part parents have to play as their child's first educators, and as equal partners with pre-school settings and other services.

Parental involvement – refers to the active inclusion of parents in shaping and evaluating services and programmes.

Community involvement – refers to the active inclusion of representatives of the communities served by children's centres in shaping and evaluating services and programmes.

In each of these cases partnership is seen as all those working together to develop and plan do so as equal members of the team. All views are valued and everyone is listened to.

Social inclusion – is taken to mean that all people are valued and treated equally, with every attempt made to make services accessible and staff approachable. Needs are recognised as offering opportunities rather than barriers.

Professional heritage – refers to the embedded practices, language and ethos of individual professions which individuals who join become familiar with as they gain experience and progress within the parameters of the profession. These are sometimes explicit but are often so deeply embedded that they are not perceived by members of the profession. In partnership working it is essential to acknowledge the way professional heritage affects points of view, language and perceptions of situations.

Identifying needs and how to address them

The term 'needs' and how needs are perceived by those involved requires some consideration itself. The government categorises the needs of communities according to 'indices of deprivation', which then indicate high, medium or low levels of need. The index is calculated from National Census data and information from local authorities, providing an indication of need and some kind of basis for the government's use of terms such as 'vulnerable' to describe families and communities. Individuals may see things differently and may well not see themselves as 'vulnerable'. Individuals have an immediate and personal perception of need, described by Maslow (1943) as a 'hierarchy of need' starting with the need to acquire the basics in order to survive, such as nutrition, shelter and clothing, through safety, the need for love and belonging, to personal aspiration and fulfilment. While these perspectives are connected, matching those as perceived by the government (top down) with those as perceived by communities, families and children (bottom up) is complex. This complexity is increased as local authorities, professions and agencies contribute their own perspectives and needs to the mix. The fact that those involved may disagree with direction, priority or emphasis compounds the challenge.

In this respect children's centres have a key role in engaging with children and families to discover what their needs are and with professionals and agencies in order to match service provision to those needs.

 Points for reflection

How would you define 'needs' in the context of partnership working?

Whose needs should be considered?

Whose needs should come first?

Identifying needs: listening to the community

The publication of *Every Child Matters: Change for Children* (DfES, 2004) signalled a clear intention for partnership to more fully include parents. The document sets out the government agenda with timescales and targets as they relate to parents. There is a clear, explicit expectation for agencies to cooperate at all levels (*Every Child Matters* 1.2, p.4). The range of coverage includes pre-school and school as well as Health, and there is a focus on reconfiguring services around the family and children, as well as improving services themselves and the way in which they integrate to provide more universal services. The role of children's centres and extended schools in bringing together integrated teams and in providing single locations for services is a clear aim. There is recognition of the need for skilled and 'enterprising' leadership at all levels and a desire to develop a 'shared sense of responsibility' across all agencies involved in child protection. Significantly there is an expectation that children, young people and families will be listened to before services are planned or delivered. While there is much here that is commendable, there are some issues that are glossed over, not least that children's centres and extended schools are mentioned in the same sentence almost as if they were equivalent, which they are not. This is discussed more fully later in this chapter and in Chapter 6. Nevertheless, there remains the clear expectation that the agencies involved will listen and work with families and each other in a much more fully integrated way.

The publication of *Every Parent Matters* in 2007 provided equally clear expectations of all involved. Not all agencies view the inclusion of parents from the same perspective or approach working with them on an equal basis. Attitudes are deeply embedded in professional heritages and will take time to change. When they are included as equals, parents' contributions are as creative as any producing a strong sense of achievement. This is explored in depth in Whalley et al. (2007) and echoed in comments from a children's centre leader in April 2008 regarding the most satisfying aspects of partnership working:

> ... satisfying parents and children's needs such as knowing the family has now got extra income; knowing that positive outcomes have been reached as a result of the partnership; to successfully reach goals as a joint initiative ...

Powell explores the difficulties inherent in the 'hierarchies of communication and participation' (Nurse, 2007: 25) and the problem of perspectives which tend to ignore the parent and the child. The appointment of a Children's Commissioner shows some progress but still leaves many traditional systems in place which tend to impose their will rather than respond to the desires or will of either children or parents.

Positive and balanced partnership can be difficult to establish for other reasons. A children's centre leader provided an example of a parent and service users group which became dominated by a powerful individual. The imbalance destroyed a great deal of work that had gone into setting up the group, damaged relationships with other agencies and service providers, and undermined the positive work being undertaken with less vocal or confident individuals and families. The centre leader had an uncomfortable and difficult time challenging the individual and re-establishing a more healthy, open and genuinely representative group. Successful partnership requires willingness of all involved to value each other's perspectives. It cannot be achieved if any single member seeks to dominate.

> There is also some slight evidence ... that commitment to parental participation and involvement, as well as to children's rights to participation, varied across type of setting and might reflect the very different aims, purpose and origins of different early childhood services as well as the different needs of the client groups serviced.
>
> (Aubrey, 2007: 37)

Anecdotal evidence from the research conducted for this book suggests that the way individuals perceive and articulate their own needs can be very different: agencies working with families and communities may have to disentangle the external symptoms, signs and emotional responses before clearer visions of need can be achieved. These internal needs require skilled and patient individuals to work with service users themselves, children, families and communities in order to articulate and describe them. There remains a tension between services that are deemed to be required to address national trends, such as the emphasis on breastfeeding babies, healthy eating or reduction in smoking, and those identified by the users themselves. The evidence from the research suggests that balancing these needs is important if settings are to achieve their core aim of being inclusive and for service users to achieve a sense of ownership. Working with service users is essential if their priorities are to be identified and relevant services provided. In the survey which underpins the most recent perspectives quoted in this book, one children's centre leader commented that what contributes to successful practice is:

> Listening to the needs of the community; taking the needs of the community to address the gaps; asking others to help and not to solve problems before others are involved. (Children's centre leader)

Covey (2004: 240) describes four levels of listening: ignoring, pretending, selective and attentive, then adds a fifth, empathetic listening. He suggests that listeners are too often 'filled with our own rightness, our own autobiography'. The examples provided suggest this is also true of organisations as much as individuals.

The examples which follow in this chapter set out what is being achieved by closer partnership with service users. They also indicate the skill areas in which professionals need to establish trust and to balance providing help and support, with enabling individuals and families to help themselves.

The setting quoted above provided the following example, which shows that being well intentioned alone is not enough.

 Case study

Getting active

A setting wanted to provide an activity for children at risk of becoming obese so that parents would also be encouraged to take part. They developed a programme with health visitors and sports coaches from local schools. Children were to be referred by parents to health visitors but there was very little take-up of places despite obesity being an issue in local schools. On reflection they realised it was probably seen by some as a fat camp: children did not want to be identified and parents did not want to take part.

The setting staff began a process of review looking at including suitable activities to support children in danger of becoming obese within the normal holiday activity programme. This they hoped would be more successful.

This example shows how important it is to think through ideas before they are put in place to avoid negative responses. The example also illustrates the degree of subtlety required when providing services to meet a specific need, such as maintaining a healthy weight, where an indirect approach, for example by a 'fitness and fun' activity, could avoid labelling individuals who take part.

 Points for reflection

What can be learnt about planning services to meet needs from examples such as this?

How would you approach this issue?

Which other agencies do you think might usefully be involved in addressing issues linked with obesity?

How might unpopular labelling be avoided by more innovative service provision?

Working in partnership with parents

Government policy has gradually increased the emphasis on partnership with parents, as the Foreword to *Every Parent Matters* demonstrates (DfES, 2007):

> Government wants to support the development of a wide range of services for parents to access as and when they need to. At the same time, we want to empower parents to influence and shape public services such as schools, health and children's services, as part of our public service reforms.
>
> (Alan Johnson, Secretary of State for Work and Pensions)

Parents were specifically included in the Sure Start Local Programmes and in practice partnership boards built on the work of EYDCPs. In many cases parent sub-boards were an important medium for getting to the heart of 'insider' perspectives and needs (Anning and Ball, 2008: 23) and helped overcome the feelings among parents of not being equal. Initially these forums and parent participation were compromised when local authorities took over control of Sure Start programmes. Although there was parent representation on steering groups for children's centres, these served a different function. Many settings have been creative in encouraging parents to come together in groups and forums to discuss issues and needs and comment on services. This proved very useful in generating ideas and approaches. The following boxed examples illustrate how two settings approached wider consultation through their parents' forum.

Parents' forum

Commissioning projects to work with us at the centre has proved beneficial to families. The Parents' Forum has been successful as parents took responsibility for deciding the layout of the children's play area and the colour scheme of the new capital build. A full consultation process commenced with parents taking the lead to gain views from other parents and children.

Consultation with children is normally carried out by their key person who can enlist the help of parents or carers. With young children consultation can be through observation, with the adult identifying what signals the child gives to show pleasure or displeasure and which activities or objects they enjoy or ignore. In some cases cameras have been used to capture moments when a child is engrossed or deeply engaged.

Consultation in this case enabled the parents to be actively involved in arriving at a decision and in seeking the views of others. Some settings have trained parents as 'ambassadors' within the community as a first step in seeking wider views. The next example shows the effect such consultation can have and how it is vital if families and individuals are to feel genuinely valued and believe they are working *with* centres rather than decisions 'done to' them.

The effect of consultation

Following the consultation with the local community a well baby clinic has been established at the centre, alongside the stay & play session, a baby group and baby cafe, and a smoking cessation session, all on Friday morning. The partners involved in setting up and running these services include health workers, children's centre workers and new leaf & district community nutritional assistants. All aspects of the partnership working to develop services were agreed and planned in the 'being healthy, staying safe' focus group for meeting the Every Child Matters agenda through integrated working.

In these cases consultation ensured that the services provided matched local needs, that they were in appropriate formats and at suitable times of the day, and had a focus and content that were a closer match to what the service users wanted. The agencies included in the consultation covered a good range of those actively involved in the community. This is much closer to the Sure Start Children's Centre description, which refers to children's centres as 'service hubs' allowing children and families easy access to information about integrated services and to 'affordable, flexible, high-quality childcare', as part of a ten-year improvement strategy (DfES, 2004b).

 Points for reflection

Why might there be reluctance by some professionals to include parents as equal partners?

How might parents themselves feel?

How might this be overcome?

As well as using staff or leaders to go out and gather opinions in face-to-face contact, settings have used opportunities for parents and service users to express their views at open days or through the evaluation of courses. Other centres have trained parents as researchers to assess the value of newly established services, as the next example indicates.

 Case study

Parents as researchers

Between 2003 and 2004 a researcher was commissioned by separate Sure Start programmes in two different Midlands local authorities to run training in research theory and practice for parents and a mixed group of parents and staff. It was challenging for the parents and for the researcher but over time the parents' confidence improved as they learnt the theory and practice of research skills and were empowered to undertake 'real' research for their programmes. The trained groups conducted surveys which provided data for future planning at their respective centres. The parents' sense of achievement at the end of the programme was immense.

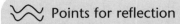 Points for reflection

If partnership working is complex and challenging for professionals how must it seem to parents and the wider community?

What benefits are there for them from engaging in the services on offer?

The widening range of partners and levels of partnership

Consulting and working with parents takes courage, skill, time and care. The same is true of consulting and working with a wide range of partner agencies and although this has become a more established part of children's centre working, it is no less demanding. In Chapter 3 there is an indication of the range of partner agencies. The examples below were provided by children's centre leaders in April 2008. They indicate available services and the level of partnership working. Each of the groups from the most to the least well developed partnerships is a mixture of statutory and user-requested service providers. The quality often depends on how long the service has been running but more particularly on the individuals involved, their degree of commitment and the quality of their working relationship. The level of partnership for Health appears to be generally high but Social Welfare is variable and Education is only specifically included in one example. Services involving a direct parent partnership appear to be working at a more highly developed state of partnership.

Children's centre partners

Setting 1

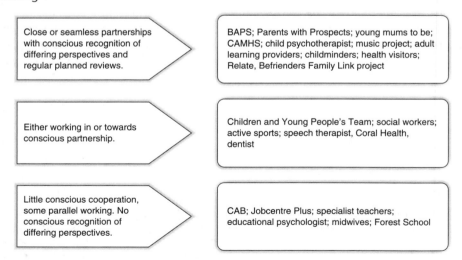

Figure 5.1   Children's centre partners – Setting 1

Setting 1 has a large number of advanced partnerships which imply complex arrangements. At the other end of the scale the low level partnerships include some important professionals.

Setting 2

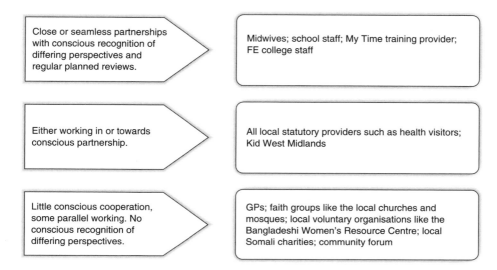

Figure 5.2   Children's centre partners – Setting 2

Setting 2 has additional requirements across all services in terms of allowing equal access, particularly to individuals and groups disadvantaged by language and cultural differences as well as by economic and social circumstances. However, their advanced partnerships include professional groups where such close working was not present in Setting 1.

Setting 3

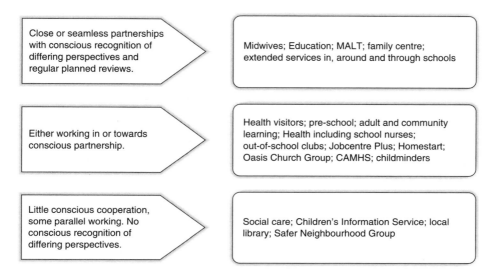

Figure 5.3   Children's centre partners – Setting 3

Setting 3 appears to have more developing partnerships but as with Setting 2 also includes advanced partnerships with groups not working at that level in Setting 1.

Setting 4

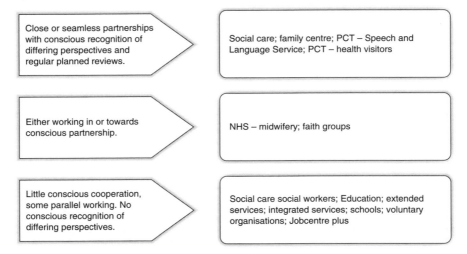

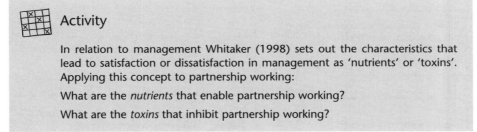

Figure 5.4   Children's centre partners – Setting 4

Setting 4 shows a reversal of partnership development compared with the others and emphasises the local variations existing in the degree and quality of partnership working, even between centres and agencies representing key partners in centre core services. All the examples reveal the challenge for centre staff and leaders in terms of the skills they need to manage basic communication between themselves and such diverse partners. An issue for many centres is how to manage consultation meetings as the points of contact begin to expand, yet maintain clear communication, allowing everyone an equal voice.

Activity

In relation to management Whitaker (1998) sets out the characteristics that lead to satisfaction or dissatisfaction in management as 'nutrients' or 'toxins'. Applying this concept to partnership working:

What are the *nutrients* that enable partnership working?

What are the *toxins* that inhibit partnership working?

Success stories from practice: benefits for children and families

The case studies below provide clear examples of benefits to families from their contact with a children's centre.

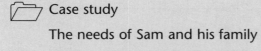 Case study

The needs of Sam and his family

Sam is referred for a priority placement in the nursery by speech and language therapists who are concerned about his delayed development. Sam's parents both have learning difficulties and are supported by a health visitor and community mental health worker. The nursery has a Designated Special Provision for children with speech and language difficulties. A speech therapist works part-time in the nursery (under a service level agreement with the NHS).

Nursery staff and the speech therapist visit Sam and his family at home, prior to his starting at the nursery.

Sam's parents ask the nursery to arrange transport into the nursery for Sam, as the family live some seven miles away. They are badly in need of some respite time. The relationship between the parents is at risk.

Sam's transition into the nursery is a confusing time for him. He lashes out at the adults in the nursery, spitting at and hitting them and throwing toys and equipment. Staff bringing Sam into the nursery refuse to collect him after a few difficult weeks when Sam throws things, bites, scratches and screams. The nursery SENCO manages to reinstate the transport by suggesting that one of Sam's parents acts as an escort on the school bus. Sam finally settles well.

Nursery staff invite health visitors, mental health workers, the educational psychologist and an advisory teacher to a mid-term review meeting. A family support plan is agreed, involving support from: the health visitor, the mental health worker, nursery staff and a children's centre family support worker.

After some six months in the nursery, Sam is making very good progress. The children's centre workers support the family in a series of visits to local primary schools to enable them to consider their ultimate choice of school for him. Nursery staff support the family with regular informal information about ways to support his learning. One family support worker works with the family using a video recorder to highlight particularly successful interactions between Sam and his parents. There are advantages to Sam, his family and the community: Sam's parents have been helped to maintain positive relationships and to support Sam's learning and development. Sam has made very good developmental progress. Nursery staff have been challenged but ultimately affirmed in their practice.

The success of this case study lies in the way in which the children's centre staff managed the initial issues and then acted as coordinators to enable access to a range of relevant professionals. While in the past assistance for Sam and his family might have eventually been found it may well have taken longer; success would have depended on someone taking the lead and communication being maintained. The children's centre provides coordination and contacts to enable the process to come together sooner, to be less threatening to the family and to be fully supportive over time. More importantly, the centre also provides the basis for underlying trust to be established, without which little can be achieved of lasting value.

In this case there are also clear benefits to the professional agencies involved, with the children's centre acting as coordinator and providing a forum to discuss the family's needs and how best to meet them. Without this the agencies might well end up failing to really meet those family needs. The trust between the centre and agencies is also key to developing successful partnership working and confidence (Fitzgerald and Kay, 2008: 11; Bertram et al., 2002: 108).

These themes are also reflected in the next case study.

Case study

New to the community

A family had recently moved to England, mum did not speak English and had a new baby, a 5-year-old and 2-year-old. During a home visit the health visitor was very concerned about the safety of the baby, the standard of health in making the feeds and the behaviour of a 5-year-old who was not in school. The family did not have a pushchair so could not take the children out, and they had no toys and very little money. The health visitor spoke to me [Head of Children's Centre] and we arranged a multi-agency meeting with the following positive outcomes:

- A pushchair was borrowed from the children's resource centre.
- An interpreter was arranged to visit the family with a community nursery nurse who gave mum some guidance and support on making up feeds for the baby.
- The interpreter and nursery nurse assisted mum to complete the admission forms for school – the 5-year-old started school and two sessions of respite were offered for the 2-year-old.
- An appointment was made with Welfare Rights and a referral was made for Safe and Healthy Homes.

This shows how the quality of contacts developed by the children's centre benefitted all members of a vulnerable family, and the prompt, coordinated action by a network of services meant each of the children and their parents was able to make a better start. The provision of equipment improved the mother's ability to get out and about, while the access to translating skills meant understanding could begin where previously there had been anxiety, fear and confusion, and assisted the family's introduction to other relevant services. The quality of relationships, trust and respect between service providers and parents are key to success, as reflected by Sure Start (Anning and Ball, 2008: 62ff.).

Outreach services have a particularly valuable part to play in meeting and establishing contact with families in need, like the family in the example above. They are often the first point of contact and a great deal depends on the quality and sensitivity of that contact. In some cases the first point of contact may be from another family or agency but in most cases the centre outreach teams have the responsibility of initiating contact and supporting the family's induction into the centre. The following case study illustrates the role and importance of children's centre outreach services as important points of contact for families and the community.

 Case study

Healthy baby

A health and family support team worker Bharti came into contact with a woman, identified as Surinder. This occurred while she was working alongside the health visitors as part of their weekly weighing clinic. Surinder was a lady from an Asian background who spoke little English. She had two children, a baby aged 7 months and an older child aged 2 years. She was attending the clinic to have the baby weighed. Concerns were raised when the baby was found to be underweight. At this time Bharti introduced herself to the woman and spoke to her in Urdu/Punjabi. With the woman's permission she arranged to visit her at home where she could spend time with her discussing aspects of feeding and weaning relevant to the baby's health. This visit was carried out within a few days, at which time Bharti signed the family up to Sure Start and gained a comprehensive history of the younger child's current eating habits. She found that the baby was still being given 5/6 milk feeds a day with very little solids included. She then gave a detailed health promotion, suggesting a reduction of the number of milk feeds given daily, and the introduction of more solids incorporating a variety of food types appropriate to the family culture, such as vegetables, fruit, cereals, roti, dhal and rice pudding. She also suggested ways to make mealtimes an enjoyable experience for the child, including sitting at the table with other family members, where currently the child was fed alone and at different times to the rest of the family. This was to be combined with different ways to introduce new tastes and textures, such as doing role play with the children based on mealtimes, a teddy bear's picnic and so on, arrived at by discussion and by practical advice. More exercise was encouraged so that the child would have more energy and feel more hungry. Bharti supported the discussion by providing information leaflets to reiterate what had been discussed, which she gave to other family members, the purpose being to involve the whole family in the exercise, and for them to read it to the mother who was unable to read herself.

By the time Bharti met Surinder at the next weighing clinic the baby had gained weight and continued to do so at each of the following attendances.

These case studies and examples begin to give an idea of the value that partnership working provides for children and families. Research by Weinstein et al. (2003) writing from a social work perspective showed that preventative work by housing, education and healthcare services can lead to better outcomes for children. This work also showed the value of consultation with parents and children when planning services and the value of empowering parents and helping them improve their parenting skills. Developing trust was also found to be critical but this can be compromised when the welfare and safety of children take priority. Ensuring that partnership policies support and do not undermine individual relationships was another key aspect (Weinstein et al., 2003: 157–8).

More information is provided in the National Evaluation of Sure Start (NESS, 2004: part 1 and part 2) and Bertram et al. (2002). In general terms partnership working enables:

- the identification of specific needs of children and families;
- improved access to regular childcare and education;
- availability of a wider range of services;
- better access to services;
- support aimed at empowering individuals to take responsibility for themselves;

roved well-being and self-esteem;

- reduction in the worst effects of poverty and ultimately reduction in poverty itself.

Benefits for professionals

It sounds logical and reasonable that more coordination in services for children, families and communities would avoid confusion and repetition of simple tasks, improve access to relevant help, advice and services and provide greater satisfaction for professionals. When professional agencies manage to coordinate successfully, those needing help can access many professionals at one time, rather than having to approach each separately, several times over. Initial dialogue and discussion between service providers can enable better understanding of each other's perspectives, knowledge and skills can be shared, and joint planning of new projects can benefit from the improved understanding, trust and shared information. Where there is inclusion of service users in the dialogue, this brings a vital perspective and helps ensure that what is provided is relevant and appropriate, as well as adding to the empowerment of the individuals (Anning and Ball, 2008: 166; DfES, 2002: 106).

In the Weinstein et al. example quoted above the risk of agencies undermining each other is a key reason for developing partnership working: it represents a fundamental fear of all potential partners, not just of social workers, and needs to be understood by all the other potential partner agencies who are each conscious of the quality of their relationship with the child, family or community in question. Dialogue and shared experience are a means to develop and improve the level of shared understanding and of maintaining the best quality relationship with all relevant agencies.

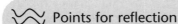 Points for reflection

How can groups of professionals be brought together?

Who should take responsibility for leading this?

How can all involved be reassured that team and partnership working will improve service planning, delivery and outcomes?

Partnership working is a way of taking in the bigger picture and providing clearer focus and maximum effectiveness of resources to meet the needs of children, families and communities rather than each agency doing their own thing. The case studies above show how children's centres can be the catalyst for drawing agencies together. The trust established by the centre provides an introduction to other agencies which might have taken much longer to establish by the family on their own, if indeed they could have managed it at all. This is shown clearly in practice by the example of Camden (see Chapter 1). Chapter 3 explored how different countries approach ECEC service organisation and provision. The example set by the Scandinavian countries and New Zealand shows what can be achieved for young children and families through a more joined up approach, including the planned provision of adequate funding by government.

Professionals can learn a great deal from each other through dialogue focused on specific needs. Misconceptions, assumptions and negative experiences can be overcome if the relationships are fostered and encouraged positively. Through work on the NPQICL programme it has been fascinating to see adults with differing professional heritages approach common tasks and acknowledge how their understanding of other professions has grown and matured. While each retains their own professional skills, extending their appreciation and understanding of others adds a new dimension to their thinking and planning.

Covey (2004: 188–9) describes the value of 'the emotional bank account' between people and argues that it improves where there is an understanding of each other, where the little things are addressed, where commitments are adhered to, where expectations are clear, where personal integrity is demonstrated and where sincere apology is made when a person makes a 'withdrawal' from the account. This reflects many of the aspects of the relationships between children's centre key persons, service providers and families extended to interprofessional relationships. It is hard to establish and maintain this level of relationship within and between partnership teams, where professional heritage can create powerful barriers.

Getting these valuable principles in relationships between professional agencies right can improve the quality of understanding and enable improved partnership working. Dialogue with other agencies can help us to better understand aspects of our own professional heritage and perspectives (Anning et al., 2006) and how our professional and personal predispositions affect working relationships within our own professional relationships as well as those with others. There are still uncertainties about the most effective parent body: Anning and Ball (2008: 164ff.) suggest that the Sure Start Local Programmes run by Health were more effective than those run by Education. (Issues arising from the move to locate more children's centres on school sites and for control to be vested in local authority bodies responsible for Education are explored further in Chapter 6.) The following example describes how a head teacher helped to develop an informal system of support for vulnerable families by working in close cooperation with colleagues from other agencies.

 Case study

Getting in touch

The head teacher had grown to understand more clearly the value of dialogue with other professionals focused on children and families who were in need of support. The head teacher was very frustrated at attending case conferences where the professional group were usually faced with having to make the least worst choice. In discussion with colleagues from Social Services and Health, he discovered they shared this frustration and concluded that it would be much better if intervention could be offered at an earlier stage. It might even avoid the need for a case conference which tended to be a blunt instrument at best. Together they identified a core of families who kept appearing at case conferences where the group thought (a) they might be prepared to talk and (b) the group could offer possible help. The group worked out which among them or other professionals had the best quality relationship and agreed that whatever might happen the core relationship must not be damaged. It was the sheet anchor and too important to risk. The group

(Continued)

members were apprehensive that no one would take up the offer or, if they came to a meeting, would not want the help offered. Their fears were unfounded and all those approached initially agreed to meet and welcomed help. The group was able to help most of the families make significant improvements over time. It was not straightforward and there were relapses but the achievements gradually overtook the downturns. As professionals the group learnt a great deal about what could be achieved, about what each had to offer and about what was beyond their spheres of influence. It was risky in the sense that they had no official status or approval. The initial agreement that no one should be asked to infringe what they considered to be confidentiality was successful and all worked around potentially difficult areas. There was a shared sense of excitement instead of a sense of frustration and a sense of achievement over time.

The benefits to professionals in this example reflect those found in other situations: they are to do with personal understanding and confidence, insights into each professional's own professional paradigms, better understanding of other professionals who can become close working colleagues, and improved sharing of information, planning and training. This was indicated by Bertram et al. (2002: 95) who reported the following benefits for professionals of integrated working:

- improvement in professional competence for Early Years workers, particularly from the private and voluntary sectors;

- increased integrated service experience for a range of practitioners;

- improved qualification levels for Early Years workers at all levels, from unqualified to graduate and beyond;

- enhanced opportunities for volunteer involvement for parents and other members of the local community.

Clark and Waller (2007: 11) refer to concerns expressed by Sylva and Pugh and in the *Starting Strong* report (OECD, 2001), regarding the expansion of Early Years policy in the UK, among which is a concern over staff training and the limiting aspects of multi-agency working such as differentials in terms of employment and salaries (also referred to by Bertram et al.). Kagan and Hallmark, quoted in Baldock et al. (2005: 86), refer to key areas of skill for Early Years leaders: administrative, pedagogical leadership, leading community services and initiatives, advocacy for groups and political awareness. The increased government emphasis on leadership in Early Years has enabled progress in training leaders through the NPQICL programme and the introduction of EYPS. Terms of employment and pay and conditions within children's centres have been reviewed in some local authorities, but there is much more to be done. These aspects are explored more fully in Chapters 6 and 7. What is important here is that where action has been taken the results have been positive. Hopefully the emerging regional support networks for children's centre leaders will provide an additional forum for debate, dialogue and mutual support.

As coordinator of the research to evaluate the Early Excellence Centre (EEC) programme I worked closely with EEC leaders. Over the period of time we worked together from 1999 to 2004 it was fascinating to see the growth in confidence, belief in what centres themselves were doing, improvements to practice and organisation, and the value of the dialogue generated in network meetings facilitated by two very experienced practitioners. These sessions identified and clarified the needs in terms of identifying best practice, identifying improvements in planning and delivery of services and training needs. There is still a positive and valuable model in the way the EEC and SSLP (Sure Start Local Programmes) developed and networked, and a great deal of positive research findings provided by practitioner researchers to show the value of partnership working that is well planned and adequately resourced (NESS, 2008; Anning and Ball, 2008; Bertram et al., 2001).

 Points for reflection

What difference does it make which is the 'parent body' responsible for children's centres?

What advantages are there for children's centre leaders to have local and regional support groups separate from their employing body?

How important is it for leaders to be able to have open professional dialogue with partners?

Benefits for local communities

There is evidence of increasing consultation with and involvement of local communities in the design, provision and evaluation of ECEC services (Whalley et al., 2007; NESS, 2008; OECD, 2006a). In many cases the process of consultation has proved difficult and community reactions have been suspicious and even hostile, until trust and partnership has developed. An aspect that did not help initially concerned the transfer of Sure Start Local Programmes to other local authority departments, which meant the dissolution of existing parent and user forums and the transfer of governance to either school governors or to newly created governing bodies, with a different attitude to parental and community involvement. Initially this created resentment, particularly where parent and community forums were strong and well established, and fears of a return to policies that gave with one hand and took away with another. However, centre leaders have been keen to re-establish or maintain parental and community partnership, in many cases ensuring that representation has been maintained on steering committees. Where partnership has been developed the gains to communities can be immense, as shown in Chapter 4, Table 4.1.

Not all services will be available to all communities all of the time. While many are statutory they may not be known to parents or families and may not have existing points of contact within a community. Partnership working helps to improve communication and to demystify processes. It helps to provide easier and better coordinated access to training for life skills and for employment. Agencies are more aware of what is available and can help individuals and groups to introduce themselves to the appropriate providers. More effective communication means that there is less duplication of services and better timing. Just as individuals can feel improvement in confidence and well-being, so too can communities. Whalley et al. (2007: 3–5) set out clearly how the Pen Green philosophy has been built on community involvement. Draper and Duffy, in Pugh and Duffy (2007: 155), describe the Thomas Coram Children's Centre approach to parent partnership and hint at the benefits to the wider community. The inclusive approaches adopted by these two settings, and others which have led the shift in practice towards partnership working, have had a wide ranging influence on ECEC practitioners from the 1980s which still continues. Communities which have been included as equal partners have felt more valued and empowered to contribute to planning.

Benefits for the country as a whole

The value of dialogue as a creative, dynamic medium has been demonstrated since Socrates. In the context of multi-agency working it helps generate new ideas, indicates future needs and directions for all partners, service users and professionals, and supports strategic planning and development. When the dialogue is between a variety of professional agencies motivated to contribute positively, the potential for creativity is even greater. Partnership working is a creative process which has been used to implement national policy through the focus on design of strategies to achieve policy aims and their implementation at local level. Many individuals and agencies involved in ECEC service provision have felt more valued and confident and the national status of ECEC working has improved dramatically in the last 15 years. There are now national forums for debate and discussion. The government recognises and supports the value of ECEC services and has achieved significant progress in improving the UK profile (OECD, 2006a). National training programmes are underpinning the improvement of qualification levels among ECEC staff and increasingly children's centre leaders are finding themselves leading and contributing to partnership groups for initiatives such as the developing 'extended schools' programme. While the underlying motivation for these improvements is still open to debate, there is no doubt that the changes in UK ECEC noted by the OECD (2006a) report reflect areas and aspects where the process has been significantly influenced by multi-agency working.

 Points for reflection

How far has your experience matched the claimed benefits?

Are there examples from your own experience that you can reflect on?

Summary

The key points to remember from this chapter are as follows:

- Partnership working can benefit all involved, children, parents, practitioners and agencies, whether professional, private or voluntary.
- To work well it requires those involved to respect each other's perspectives, to be open to ideas, to listen as well as talk, to be willing to contemplate change.
- Personal honesty and acceptance of others as equals are fundamentally important.
- Valuing contributions from children, parents and communities is at the heart of partnership working.

- It is important to balance needs identified by children, parents and communities with national agendas to improve health and well-being.

The chapter has also explored:

- the gains from an open rather than a closed approach;

- the value of dialogue which provides insights into a professional's own pre-dispositions and the benefits to each group – children, parents, families and communities – using case studies and examples from practice;

- the increase in range and quality of services which can be made accessible to children, parents, families as a whole and the communities in which they live, where these issues are successfully managed.

Further reading

The following provide discussion of benefits based on examples from practice:

- Anning, A. and Ball, M. (2008) *Improving Services for Young Children: From Sure Start to Children's Centres.* London: Sage.

- Aubrey, C. (2008) *Leading and Managing in the Early Years.* London: SAGE.

- Pugh, G. and Duffy, B. (eds) (2007) *Contemporary Issues in the Early Years,* 4th edn. London: SAGE.

- Whalley, M. and the Pen Green Centre Team (2007) *Involving Parents in Their Children's Learning,* 2nd edn. London: Paul Chapman.

Useful websites

- www.everychildmatters.gov.uk/

- www.ness.bbk.ac.uk/

- www.teachernet.gov.uk/_doc/11184/6937_DFES_Every_Parent_Matters_FINAL_PDF_as_published_130307.pdf

- www.togetherforchildren.co.uk

The following link is for a report on parents' views of children's centre services carried out in the autumn of 2008:

- publications.dcsf.gov.uk/eOrderingDownload/DCSF-RB083.pdf

To find out more about Abraham Maslow's original paper:

- Maslow, A. H. (1943) 'A theory of human motivation', *Psychological Review,* 50(4): 370–96.

Or go to:

- www.businessballs.com/maslow.htm

Leadership and management issues in multi-agency settings

This chapter focuses on the changes that partnership working demands in practice, particularly in terms of the leadership and management requirements. Consideration is given to:

- the challenge of change;
- national agendas and local centre priorities;
- flexible working and responding to need in local authorities and children's centres;
- children's centres and schools: key differences affecting partnership working;
- leadership and management – how do they differ?
- leadership styles – emotional intelligence;
- identifying needs.

The challenge of change

Change is something which is exciting and challenging (see also Chapters 2 and 4). It can be also menacing to us, particularly when it threatens to disturb our carefully nurtured comfort zones. Goleman comments:

> People who lack adaptability are ruled by fear, anxiety and a deep personal discomfort with change.

> (1999: 98)

What we seem to need is contradictory: we like the security and structure of comfort zones and are threatened by change but we are also inspired and excited by new ideas and possibilities (Csikszentmihalyi, 1995).

National agendas and local and centre priorities

The tensions between national agendas and their implementation at local and setting level are passed on as challenges to be faced by Early Years care and education. Baldock et al. comment:

One thing that has been clear from the start of the implementation of the Every Child Matters strategy is that local authorities were in line for the bulk of the structural and cultural change and that this would take place mainly within existing budgets. (2005: 77)

The funding for new initiatives after 1997 was generous, allowing an initial expansion, when even local authorities not in sympathy with the government's aims found it relatively easy to begin to approach change. In line with the guidelines of Every Child Matters: Change for Children, many local authorities reorganised their departments to reflect the move towards more joined-up thinking and practice. For example, Birmingham now presents information for children, young people and families on its 'Grid for Learning' website and Islington has its own multi-agency team within the 'Policy and Performance Service'. However, funding was reduced over time and for Sure Start programmes ended in March 2008. This has meant all settings having to focus on core services and being creative in matching staffing needs to cover them. There was always a need to plan for 'sustainability', but while some settings worked towards it from the outset others did not. More recent changes and further reductions in funding have tested children's centres, ability to deliver 'core services' (see Figure 6.1) with qualified staff led by competent and efficient leaders within existing budgets.

Activity

Figure 6.1 provides a list of 'core offer' features: can you create a list of the services to match the core offer?

What kind of skills would be needed to establish and maintain the 'core offer'?

One way of reducing costs has been for local authorities to group centres in 'clusters' (Bertram et al., 2002: 40) with one leader responsible for several sites and a range of staff, often employed and line managed by different partner organisations. The demands this kind of organisation makes on staff and leaders are not always

---

North Somerset Council Children's Centres must offer access to the following core services:

- Family support
- Links to child and family health
- Outreach and home visiting
- Information and access to wider services
- Childminder's network
- Parental involvement
- Drop-in sessions for parents and children, e.g. Stay & Play
- Links to Jobcentre Plus

In addition to these services South Weston, Ashcombe, Crockerne and Central Weston Children's Centres also provide early years provision and access to education, training and employment opportunities.

www.n-somerset.gov.uk/Education/Early+years/Childrens+Centres/coreservicesofferedbychildrens centres.htm

---

Figure 6.1 One example of 'core offer' as presented by a local authority website when Phase I Children's Centres were first established. (Note: this website has since been updated.) Reproduced with Permission from North Somerset Council of Children's Services.

understood by other partners or local authorities. Bertram et al. refer to the need for a 'culture change' in agencies. This recognises that not all are sympathetic to the principles underpinning children's centres and not all agencies are willing partners (Baldock et al., 2005: 78). In some cases the emphasis on the changes needed to support children's centres has cut across existing priorities and projects. In other cases personnel and organisational changes within partner organisations and local authorities have fractured continuity in the development of understanding, planning and consequently the funding of children's centres. This is on top of existing issues around differing pay rates and conditions of service for different organisations in Health, Social Services and Education for posts carrying similar responsibilities as well as the generally low rates of pay within the Early Years sector (Baldock et al., 2005: 52).

The challenge these changes present are significant (Anning and Ball, 2008: 164ff.): local authorities in England have targets to meet for the number of children's centres in their areas and the completion of the establishment of integrated services on offer by 2010; leaders of children's centres and school heads with extended services face fundamental changes in working relationships and practices. The dilemmas for local authorities are: how to establish enough centres; how to find an affordable, trained and capable leadership workforce; how to ensure high quality in care and education elements; and how to encourage multi-agency working. The frustrations and positive potential are echoed in the following comments by a children's centre head:

> ... there are a number of potentially exciting ways in which partnership working can be extremely effective if the focus is truly around the outcomes for the client. All too frequently individuals' focus is, however, masked by the need to meet targets, or numbers and professionals become 'precious' about clients.

The positive attitude which is uppermost is well illustrated by the following response by a children's centre head to the question in my research: 'What do the terms multi-agency or partnership working mean to you?'

> The genuine commitment of staff to work together to improve outcomes for children. The existence of a 'can-do' attitude in overcoming obstacles, e.g. administrative and practical. An example ... a premises officer new to the children's centre stepping in to do something overlooked by the contractor with the words 'well ... it just needs to get done by Monday and I think I can pull it off.' This attitude means the whole show runs more smoothly and parents will be able to access the centre sooner.

The development of children's centres saw progression from the initial phase 1 children's centres into phase 2, both of which were aimed at the 30 per cent most disadvantaged areas with services centred on a single building or grouped buildings with some outreach. Phase 3 centres were focused on less disadvantaged areas, with more outreach and more flexibility over the services offered. In the case of phase 3 centres there is a minimum specification for staffing equivalent to a half-time manager, a half-time administrator and a full-time family support and sessional care worker.

In establishing children's centres some authorities, such as Nottingham and Gloucester, have drawn on the expertise of existing experienced leaders to help set up their phase 2 and phase 3 sites, but there remains a shortfall in suitably experienced and qualified leaders and workforce to extend and develop settings once they are established. Less common is the use of experienced leaders, staff and service users in developing medium- and long-term strategies.

Baldock et al. (2005: 85) point to the increased expectation on centre leaders magnified by the 'managerialist approach to funding provision' adopted by the government which has increased administration and the range of targets and made the acquisition of funding a major challenge. Aubrey also points to the need for change in the understanding of leadership in the Early Years and the need for new approaches to leadership (Aubrey, 2008: 136–9). There is a danger that leaders will be overburdened and lost to the service unless their experience and expertise can be recognised, valued and drawn upon for future planning.

The announcements in the Children's Plan may go some way towards addressing these issues and to linking the care and education agendas but there is a great deal to be achieved before 2010, particularly if the shift in preferred ways of working, service identification and delivery are to be maintained and developed in a sustainable way between 2010 and 2020 (Children's Plan, DCFS, 2007). A key part of achieving the planned change is for local authority officers and administrators in each of the statutory agencies to recognise that Early Years and care services are complex, and are hindered and easily damaged by planning that remains focused on previous needs, protocols and practice no longer appropriate to new needs based on flexibility. Improving the level of knowledge and understanding within administrations is essential if partnership working is to succeed.

Government planning is partly grounded and informed by ongoing research such as the Millennium Cohort Study (MCS) (http://publications.dcsf.gov.uk/eOrdering Download/DCSF-RW077.pdf), which examines the level of achievement of a sample of children at age 5 and, inter alia, has identified strong links between the mother's education, social circumstances and tendency to depression with low achievement in their children. The report also indicates the importance of parents reading and interacting with their children and acknowledges there is movement in both directions in terms of children born in or out of poverty and their measured performance at age 5.

The Children's Plan was formed after consultation with all parties including children and families equally with professionals. The website has versions specifically designed to be accessible to families and young people. The Plan aims to improve support for families while children are young, improve education, involve parents more fully, increase 'interesting and exciting' things for young people outside school and provide safe play spaces. The strong emphasis on change is underpinned by a vision of schools as centres for local communities and an expectation that Children's Trusts will take a lead role in enabling this shift in emphasis and practice. The version for families uses more friendly language and indicates the government's intention of putting children and families at the centre, with access to improved childcare with 'more and better' childcare available and improved schools. There is a clear statement showing the link between the Children's Plan and the UN Convention on the Rights of the Child and all this information is now more readily available online.

The Plan presents a manifesto for change with a stated commitment of funding for improvements to local play facilities: 'A new national strategy on play will be backed by £225 million over three years, starting early in 2008. Every local area will get extra money by 2010' (Children's Plan, Parents and Families, p. 12). It includes improvements to health care and provision for children with additional needs as well as those living 'in poverty', aiming 'at halving child poverty by 2010 and end it by 2020' (ibid.). The role of Sure Start children's centres in providing support for parenting and 'key workers' for families is explicit. There is a commitment to continue the emphasis on high-quality pre-school services which are graduate-led (where full-time day care is offered) and accessible to all, and increase free time and places available to 3 and 4 years olds, expanding to 2 year olds in deprived areas. There is promise of change in approaches at primary level and new partnership with parents. Other sections cover plans for increased safety for children, outlining changes to encourage young people to continue in education beyond school and have better access to more activities to avoid disaffection and reduce the levels of crime and alcohol abuse in this age group.

Overall the Children's Plan brings together various government aims and by implication draws together different agencies, while retaining a heavy emphasis on education. It does acknowledge the views of parents and young people and sets up communication accessible to those who are motivated to seek it. Whether there could be a greater demonstration of joined-up thinking in action by spelling out more clearly the multi-agency opportunities and expectations, rather than being quite so heavily focused on education, remains to be seen.

Partnership working: challenges for leaders

Government have provided resources and incentives to explore and introduce change such as the Children's Plan, but a healthy balance is required: too much change risks practitioners becoming swamped by initiatives, too little risks stagnation. The fundamental issue around the need for innovation, creativity, change and flexibility on the one hand and the need for consistent form and order and structured processes and procedures on the other underpins all in practice. Administrative services are accountable and must have systems of operation that allow traceable pathways in decision-making and actions. Precedents that are set need to be sustainable, fair, consistent and as efficient as possible in terms of time, energy and cost.

Sure Start children's centres developed from practice promoting innovation and creativity. Unfortunately these aims can be hard to reconcile with the need for administrative systems meeting local authority demands for accountability and transparency. The dissonance can create conflict and there have been casualties among leaders, as the change to children's centres located in and managed by local authority education and care services has imposed conditions which children's centre leaders have found contradicted their fundamental values and principles. This has been particularly true for those from Health, Social Services and Community Development backgrounds or from private or business sectors. The tension between demands to innovate and create new systems and the need for conformity to established fiscal, procedural and governance protocols is an active dilemma for leaders of children's centres themselves and the services they provide, as well as for the administrative services to whom they are accountable. The location of Sure Start children's centres in local authority departments responsible for Education is questioned by Anning and Ball, who raise concerns over the potential damage to multi-agency and partnership working by the imposition of a dominating philosophy and practice (Anning and Ball, 2008: 167–8).

Leadership and organisation at local authority level

Leadership and management at the centre level needs the support, understanding, resources and organisation from the local authority level to perform effectively. Gardner, in Weinstein et al. (2007), sets out concerns for multi-agency working, stressing the need for more evidence to compare joint and single-agency programmes. She argues that the strength of collaboration is 'only as strong as the confidence, capacity and skills of the workforce to undertake it' and is not helped when undertaken by agencies which themselves are in a state of change or disruption. This underlines the need for more careful planning towards partnerships and improved understanding of what is required for success. Gardner points to the need for partnership working to be seen as 'a medium to long-term venture not a "quick fix"' and comments on how rushed, ill-conceived or imposed partnerships can have the opposite effect from that intended. This matches experience from local authorities where school heads have felt the reality of on-site children's centres has not matched the initial briefing and good will has been the first casualty. This is further commented on by Gardner who points to the need for strategic collaboration, understanding, leadership and vision to establish clear communication and relevant, supportive infrastructure to 'establish and sustain joint programmes and the capacity for learning, ... the engine for joint service delivery' (Gardner, in Weinstein et al., 2007: 157). There is emerging anecdotal evidence which confirms that in too many cases the lack of understanding at strategic level combined with the disruptive effects of change within authorities and agencies is resulting in ill-conceived implementation of the children's centre programme, with the negative results expressed in Gardner's concerns.

The constraints governing local authorities can inhibit partnership working. The Children's Plan target dates allow a ten-year period, longer than many government timescales but still relatively short for fundamental shifts in practice. Additional constraining factors include time fixed by external demands and reorganisation placing all local authority employees under threat and disturbing continuity. There is often little appreciation of the needs for successful partnership working by those responsible for establishing it. Target setting in local authorities can inspire or impede: Freidman (2005) argues for targets and evaluation which allow for intelligent and positive measures of success to encourage, rather than limited and inflexible targets envisaging either total success or total failure which can discourage and demotivate. Targets for partnership working need to be more creative and appropriate to the needs of the system being supported.

In some cases partnership working is seen as a means of economising. While it is true that partnership working can save money it is a mistake to see it as a cheap option (DfEE, 2000). Take, for example, a local authority where phase 2 children's

ıre all located on school sites and their leaders are all from an exclusively
ırs education background but inexperienced in leadership and new to part-
....ıp working, yet responsible for settings with the same core offer but funded at
a lower level than phase 1 settings. In this case placing children's centres on school
sites with newly promoted leaders has been a cheaper option which may have been
well intentioned but has meant in practice leaders have been given demanding
aims that equate to those of earlier centres but without their independence, funding or resources. These leaders have found themselves controlled by school systems
which were not appropriate to children's centre aims and responsible to head
teachers and governors with little understanding of what children's centres are and
who in many cases saw them as primarily a means of securing their school intake.

Well informed understanding and strong, positive leadership is required from local
authorities if partnership working is to maintain the initial impetus and develop
effectively.

 Points for reflection

How can a better understanding of what children's centres are and how they
work be developed at all levels?

How can the process of change be led and managed in a positive way?

The pressure to innovate, share information, develop new practices, be inclusive and
provide a genuine service, is increasing and is a clear government agenda (cf.
Children Act 2004, Common Assessment Framework 2006, Every Child Matters 2004,
Children's Plan 2008). Currently children's centres and extended schools programmes
are functioning in parallel, not as the potentially achievable unified whole. The Ofsted
report undertaken in 2005, based on 20 schools in 16 authorities offering extended
services, found a great deal to be positive about (Ofsted, 2006). The Key Findings
showed confirmation of benefits to children, young people and adults with
improved self-confidence, relationships and attitudes to learning. Strong leadership
linked to clear understanding of aims and willingness to include others were key factors for success, along with careful planning looking at affordability and beyond the
short term. The report drew attention to the importance of team work between agencies with a clear leader and planned support from the local authority. In addition:

> The most successful providers shaped the provision gradually to reflect their commu-
> nity's needs and wants in collaboration with other agencies. They gave sufficient time
> to gather information on local requirements before setting up any provision. There was
> no single blueprint for success. Regular consultation by services was vital. Successful
> services fulfilled the community's needs, were of high quality and maintained interest.

> Short-term funding made it difficult for services to plan strategically. This influenced sig-
> nificantly which services were provided and the extent to which they could be sustained.

(Ofsted, 2006)

The implications for leadership and management are clear. The successes have
hinged on careful planning within agreed protocols, with clear leadership by well
informed and committed professionals. The best results achieved were with consultation and an ability to respond to identified needs in a flexible way. Realistic funding

and time frames with ongoing support have been key factors for success as have the dissemination and sharing of good practice. The recognition that there is no single model for success is a strong argument for caution when local authorities are tempted by one aspect such as finance. These findings reflect the previous research and endorse the views expressed by Friedman. To achieve the levels of successful working detailed above requires considerable and diverse skills which cannot be assumed and will not happen by accident. Careful planning including all relevant parties and realistic allocation of time and funding is required. All parties need to come together as equal partners, recognising the value and contribution each brings.

Combining the care and education agendas (balancing the curriculum)

Partnership working between Social Services and Education within pre-school and Early Years has become more securely established since 1997. However, there remains concern, supported by research findings (EPPE – DfES, 1997–2004, NESS, 2005) that the cognitive and challenge aspects, set too high or too low for individual children, are not as strong as those relating to care. There needs to be clarity about the key aspects of each and they should be complementary, the warp and weft that combine to produce a new entity stronger than either individual element (OECD, 2006d: Executive Summary). European countries show two approaches to child care and education: a social model with early childhood as a preparation for life in society, and an academic model with early childhood as a preparation for formal education. The former focuses on the child, their well-being, their attitudes and their dispositions to natural learning, while the latter focuses on acquiring a set of skills and the concept of 'readiness'.

In England Education tends to be interpreted very narrowly, related more to the National Curriculum rather than Birth to Three Matters or Early Years Foundation Stage agendas. The debate in England continues over the Foundation Stage and perceived danger of a 'top-down' model. Yet there is much in the recommended approaches that expressly encourages practitioners to be open and creative, child and family centred in their approaches, rather than be constrained (see Every Child Matters, Early Years Foundation Stage). A balance is necessary. Children learn best when they are confident, curious and challenged. If their motivation is high they will persist until mastery is accomplished. Ferre Laevers work in Belgium on experiential education shows the importance of a child's involvement with the task in hand as an indicator of their focus and determination. Matching challenge to curiosity and persistence is the pedagogue's art: intervening with a question or suggestion can be critical to the child's ability to try a new strategy or build on past experience. Encouragement if a strategy in progress isn't effective is a key motivator to try again, genuine delight at success a just reward.

Together yet separate – respecting and valuing differences yet creating firmer bonds: essential differences between children's centres and schools

Increasingly children's centres are being located on school sites. This may appear logical, providing a convenient answer to surplus accommodation in schools, but there are important differences hinted at by Pugh and Duffy (2007: 18).

Children's centres have to take account of the views of the service users and adapt to meet needs as they change. Children's centres are concerned with helping people to build confidence and self-esteem and begin to take ownership of their own lives: schools are fundamentally there to educate children, following a prescribed curriculum with targeted aims and tested levels of achievement. The entire ethos, philosophy and organisation of schools are quite different from children's centres.

Traditionally schools are part of an organised, progressive system with a set curriculum and set expectations for measured progression which is inspected. They have well defined and consistent aims, a hierarchical structure, clear financial accountability, governance and inspection structures and well established routines. Although funding can vary, it tends to be predictable. While their partnership with parents has been encouraged to be more equal and inclusive, the role of parents still tends to be within clear limits, in what Epstein and Saunders refer to as a 'protective model' where responsibility for the child's education is handed over to the school; a 'school to home transmission model' where communication tends to be from the school to the home; and a 'curriculum enrichment model' with collaboration between school and parents to assist curriculum and learning (in Baldock et al., 2005: 94). There is a mixture of staff skills and training levels but with a focus on learning and teaching. Pastoral care works in parallel with the learning agenda.

Children's centres have to be flexible. They are meant to identify and respond to the needs of the families and wider community, which vary and change frequently. The care and education agendas have clear aims but the pathway to achieving them often requires innovation and is more focused on the personal and social predispositions for learning and healthy development rather than a set curriculum. Epstein and Saunders refer to this as 'partnership model' which represents a long-term commitment built on mutual respect and widespread involvement of families and practitioners (in Baldock et al., 2005). They serve different catchment areas and may include several schools although they are sited alongside or are part of one. They are focused on the needs of the whole family and staff are drawn from a wide range of professional backgrounds. Parents and adults are encouraged to be included and are treated as equals, with staff favouring a 'non-judgemental' approach to dealing with issues.

Funding tends to be unpredictable and is often from many sources. Staff providing services are often employed and line managed by agencies outside the centre itself. Leadership tends to be more of a 'flat hierarchy' or egalitarian, with an emphasis on ensuring all staff contribute and feel valued. A key premise is that the centre is there to respond to need and find ways of meeting new challenges.

The extended schools agenda provides a further complication. It was conceived at a much earlier stage than, but developed in parallel with, children's centres, yet is essentially a different agenda. The intention is to provide care beyond the school day on school sites. Groups of schools are clustered and funding is available to support these services. This presents a real challenge to schools for the reasons set out above, and while some schools have been able to develop provision others have found it is difficult to blend in this initiative just as they have had difficulty with understanding children's centres.

There are underlying values and principles which can unify schools and children's centres: many of those who are the focus for children's centres had negative experiences at school but can be coaxed to respond positively to the welcoming, non-judgemental, open atmosphere. Fundamentally the key difference is to do with attitude and atmosphere: too many formal situations, including schools, retain power and authority in what is perceived to be an authoritative, superior atmosphere which distances themselves from families; those with a more open atmosphere, whether schools or children's centres, and willingness to share or distribute power, which accept families as equals and genuinely listen, achieve a better quality contact and are better able to identify and meet needs.

Inevitably it is hard for those involved with school leadership, management and governance, who find themselves suddenly with the additional responsibility of the children's centre on site, to easily identify with its values, principles and aims or to understand the needs of the setting, staff or service users. A key challenge for all involved is to develop this understanding.

 Points for reflection

How important is it for children's centre settings on school or other sites to establish their own identity?

How does this sit alongside multi-agency working?

How can leaders include parents and carers to influence what is provided by settings? How can their 'voice' be heard as full partners?

Over time there has been a shift towards more direct contributions by parents as equal partners. While this has been a basic expectation for children's centre leaders, it has presented challenges to education leaders and to school heads, especially in terms of extended schools, even though most place partnership with parents as being second only to partnership with children. As the 2006 report on extended schools by Ofsted noted:

> The most successful providers shaped the provision gradually to reflect their community's needs and wants in collaboration with other agencies. They gave sufficient time to gather information on local requirements before setting up any provision. There was no single blueprint for success. Regular consultation by services was vital. Successful services fulfilled the community's needs, were of high quality and maintained interest.

Anecdotal evidence suggests that the reality of equal partnership varies with the leadership style of the centre or school head: to a head or leader with a more authoritarian style partnership will be on terms predetermined by them and within clearly defined limits; to a leader with a more consultative style partnership will not just allow parents more opportunity to express views, but to take real ownership and responsibility for putting those views into action. The attitude adopted by professionals has been shown to be crucial in affecting how parents and children respond. Arnold (2005) makes the point:

> The judgements made by staff or parents affect how the family feels about school and, possibly, create a barrier to becoming involved with school or education in general.

> (cited in Whalley et al., 2007: 87)

The challenge is achievable but can only happen through careful planning and specific training

Training, leadership and management

The demands on leadership have increased. Priority has been given to raising the standard of qualification in the Early Years (DfES, 2005f) and the National Professional Qualification for Integrated Centre Leadership (NPQICL), designed specifically for children's centre leaders, has begun to address a perceived gap in leadership qualifications. The Children's Workforce Development Council (CWDC) has responsibility for putting additional qualifications in place and the Early Years Practitioner Status (EYPS) is discussed in Chapter 7. What are needed are additional programmes to train aspiring leaders to raise awareness of partnership working needs and skills.

 Points for reflection

What do aspiring leaders need to be aware of?

What skills do they need to meet the complex demands on leaders, particularly in partnership working?

Leadership and management

 Activity

What is the difference between leadership and management?

Try and come up with your own definitions of each or at least a set of bullet point characteristics of each.

In her research on leadership in the Early Years, Aubrey (2007) found

> a narrow view of the leadership role, a reluctance to engage with leadership theory, a gender bias in the workforce and a relative absence of leadership development.

She quotes Ebbeck and Waniganayake (Aubrey, 2007: 28) for whom the definition of early childhood leadership 'lacked clarity, coherence and comprehension' mainly due to a failure to adapt and change. This is all the more concerning since earlier research (Rodd, 1997; Taba et al., 1999; Waniganayake et al., 2000) came to similar conclusions. This underscores the need for programmes like NPQICL which focus on issues of leadership rather than management and encourage leaders to reflect on the underpinning philosophy and values good leaders espouse. The work of the team led by Whittaker and Whalley at Pen Green in combination with NCSL Nottingham has been at the core of developing this approach. Leadership is very much about awareness of people, situations and strategies and about lasting effect or sustainability. Hargreaves and Fink (2006: 18ff.) set out seven principles of sustainable leadership covering:

- Depth, where sustainable leadership matters

- Length, where it lasts

- Breadth, where it spreads

- Justice, where it supports the environment and nurtures it

- Diversity, which is a strength

- Resourcefulness, where it develops and does not deplete resources

- Conservation, where it learns from the past for the future.

It is not necessarily about knowing everything about a situation, but having the confidence, skill and courage to look for alternative ways of taking the next step and moving forward, which may mean taking a step back. It is also about vision and being able to communicate vision and inspire or coax others to be visionary too. Essentially Early Years leadership needs to match the demands of a changing, dynamic working environment, keeping children and families at the centre of the focus.

Management on the other hand is more about systems and procedures. It is possible to be a good manager without being a good leader and vice versa. Some of the characteristics of good leadership will help improve management, for example awareness of the strengths and needs of those with whom you are working and being emotionally aware. Successful management may achieve identified targets and be inclusive, encouraging others to extend their skills and abilities by placing them in situations which are the individual's or team's to manage or deal with. Good leadership will enable the individual or team to consider ways forward and, particularly, inspire them to try out new ideas, having the confidence to risk 'failure' as a way of improving understanding and developing alternative strategies. Good budgetary management will ensure best use of funding and avoid over-spending: good leadership will encourage the kind of budgetary management which thinks beyond the immediate systems to develop creative ways of ensuring the system matches needs rather than the reverse. Charles Handy's book *The Empty Raincoat* explores changes in management and uses images to explain how the world of work and society has changed in the postmodern era. The images he describes are the 'what' of management change: leadership is the 'how'. Management requires something to manage: leadership can inspire us to boldly go where no one even knows there is somewhere to go and to create a 'something' that is meaningful and relevant to all involved.

Good leadership and good management are both required for successful organisations, especially where partnership working is a key element. The kind of leadership and management required has to be open rather than closed, aware that partners see the same scenario from different perspectives with different priorities and emphases. It has to be innovative and flexible yet find pathways and methods of organisation that are sufficiently sound and robust to deliver services while meeting the administrative and accountability needs of all partners.

Leadership style and emotional intelligence

Within multi-agency centres the style of leadership is critical to success. Research has pointed towards increased success where leaders have adopted a more inclusive, consultative style (Hargreaves and Fink, 2006; Goleman, 1999; Covey, 2004). The principles of *distributed leadership*, where responsibility for specific areas is genuinely shared (Hargreaves and Fink, 2006: 111ff.), and *flat hierarchies*, where management roles are known and respected equally and where power is not vested in one or a few individuals who impose direction, are emerging as new ways of achieving the creative demands and expectations of children's centres. These principles are grounded in a very different philosophy and value base, and require very different leadership skills that are fundamental to the development of extended schools and children's centres within local authorities. An increasing awareness of the importance of *emotional intelligence* among leaders and researchers has grown. This concept, created by Hochschild (cited in Hargreaves and Fink, 2006) and developed by Goleman (1999), has had a significant impact on the way leaders approach their work and takes into account the emotional needs of their staff, those who use their settings and themselves. The concept originally remarked on the way organisations required employees to adopt certain emotional masks, thus suppressing or hiding their real feelings, to perform their working functions. This suppression created conflict and even ill health within individuals. Goleman (1999) has shown how raising awareness of our emotions as leaders, managing them and understanding the effect on others around us improves our ability to identify with our workplace, our own roles and those of colleagues. Hargreaves and Fink include emotion as a renewing source of resourcefulness within leadership (2006: 218). Schools have introduced emotional awareness into their processes to help children and young adults to come to terms with their own emotional needs and how these affect their lives and the lives of those around them. This awareness is an important aspect of partnership working which, if present and shared by partners, can provide an essential ingredient to enable positive creativity in exploring new directions and ways of achieving them. An important first step is to establish shared values. Ira Shor (1992) set out an agenda of values for *empowering education* which, although presented as changes to pedagogic style, apply equally to the education of partners in shared partnership working. Shor advocates a style that is, inter alia, participatory, dialogic, problem-posing, democratic, multicultural and interdisciplinary (Shor, 1992: 170). These aspects are at the heart of effective partnership learning and moving towards successful partnership working.

Empowering all involved in partnership working, regardless of position or role, is a distinct challenge. A leading successful example is the work of Paulo Friere (1972) who fought to encourage underprivileged communities in Brazil to take ownership of their lives through education. Success was achieved despite a political and social system that generated a culture of dependency, conformity and acceptance of the limited quantity of knowledge and limited quality of life made available. Partnership working is very similar: the principle that all are equal and have a right to be heard and to listen, to receive full information and to have equal influence on decision-making processes potentially provides liberation for all partners, but requires a significant effort on the part of each to step outside their comfort zones, familiar frameworks and professional heritages and explore fresh possibilities together.

 Activity

Compare your description of leadership and management with the points made here. What are the similarities and differences?

Identifying partners, needs – further considerations

Chapter 4 began with a consideration of what is meant by needs and whose needs come first. Identifying needs is critical to the aims and processes of partnership working. Children's centres aim to meet the needs of children, families and communities, identified in the core offer that is provided, and decided by local authority administrators when the children's centres are set up. The leaders identify how to meet these needs and which partners to work with. The partners each meet their own needs, plus the core needs and their collective needs, in order to successfully achieve all their aims. While some of these needs may overlap, partner perceptions and ownership may not.

Identifying needs presupposes an established level of partnership plus a desire to approach issues creatively and from the bottom up. The degree to which partnerships may already be operating will vary, and the existence of 'core services' referred to earlier suggests that in most cases the initial pressure is to work from the top down. There is a presumption that the predetermined core services match the core needs of children, families and communities and are common to all areas of the country.

Gardner (2007: 157) expresses the following concern:

> While special collaboration projects and programmes can be effective, they continue to marginalize deprived children and families rather than integrate them into mainstream provision.

While government aims recognise this through the Children's Plan, success depends on establishing contact and trust with those who are marginalised and living in poverty and areas of deprivation. Effective partnership with parents at a local level is an important part of achieving aims. In their comprehensive literature review, Desforges and Abouchaar (2005) confirmed the importance and value of parental involvement in school and at home in encouraging improved performance from children and found that parental involvement increases in line with the achievements of their children. They concluded:

> The most important finding from the point of view of this review is that parental involvement in the form of 'at-home good parenting' has a significant positive effect on children's achievement and adjustment even after all other factors shaping attainment have been taken out of the equation ... The scale of the impact is evident across all social classes and all ethnic groups.

(Desforges and Abouchaar, 2003)

The effect is indirect and works through 'shaping the child's self concept' (Desforges and Abouchaar 2003: 5). It should be noted that this does not mean home mimicking school.

A key leadership function is to help all partner agencies and individuals understand and be willing to research and identify community needs. This includes local representation as equal partners on partnership boards and children's centre advisory committees while working towards meeting the predetermined targets and core services. Partnerships with open dialogue, inclusive representation, shared values and recognition of all the needs are better placed to successfully achieve this and meet the real needs of the communities they serve. In terms of parents this is reinforced by the work of Dahlberg et al. (1999), Malaguzzi (1993) and Whalley et al. (2007). Malaguzzi states:

> It is the right of parents to participate actively, and with voluntary adherence to the basic principles, in the growth, care, and development of their children who are trusted to the public institution.

> (Malguzzi, 1993)

The following case studies illustrate how this works in practice. They were provided by children's centre heads who were asked to 'provide examples as condensed case studies, which show partnership working at its best/worst from your own experience'.

 Case study

Mutual respect

Partnership working works well within the centre where we all have a good working relationship and respect each other's heritage. As we continue to build up good working relationships with other agencies the working relationship is improving.

Respect for individuals is not possible without an open-minded approach. There has to be a willingness to engage with other perspectives and associated differences in working practices and philosophies. This applies equally to working with children, parents, families and local communities. Similarly the quality of working relationships is grounded in attitudes which allow personal feelings and preferences to be moderated or set aside in order to develop improved relationships and to work towards securing understanding and trust.

Different agendas

The best example is the collaborative partnership board now developed into the advisory board. When the partnership works well together then services are much more joined up. However, in the early days of SSLP (the Sure Start Local Programme), there were partners who came to the table with additional motives such obtaining capital or revenue funding within their organisations. This led to conflict between partners when jostling for funds. At one time a board member was asked to resign as they were in danger of bringing the partnership board into disrepute.

Balancing the particular needs and agendas of individual members and agencies with the specific aims of advisory or planning groups is difficult. There is an inherent tension between the individual and the group which can become a contradiction or a synthesis. Positive leadership, which seeks to understand and take account of all parts of the dynamic that individuals bring, allowing each to feel they are listened to and valued, has a greater chance of achieving a new dynamic through inclusive dialogue. This presupposes that those involved are prepared to set aside personal preferences and agendas and understand why they are there, what it is they are trying to achieve and where the boundaries lie. For parents and community representatives the challenge to achieve their agendas is at the heart of partnership. Leaders must therefore ensure that there is clear communication and understanding.

Service level agreements have helped to structure what services are to be commissioned and what needs to be achieved by local organisations for the delivery of provision which meets the core offer. Specific, shared aims for leaders at each stage and level of partnership working ensure service level agreements setting out purpose, expectation and procedures promote a

> clear understanding of roles and responsibilities so the needs of all involved are clear. The role of local authorities was important in establishing effective, well coordinated plans and support structures. Authorities used effective settings and agencies fully to disseminate good practice.
>
> (Ofsted, 2006: 4)

While this report described extended schools it is highly relevant here. In many cases services will be commissioned by outside providers and staff involved will need careful induction into partnership aims, priorities and ways of working. This can create complex line management, where staff from a commissioned service provider agency have their own line management within their agency but are under the day-to-day leadership and management of the centre senior staff. There are other examples of greater complexity arising from shared or leased sites, rooms or sections of property. Good intentions are not enough and a poorly planned and constructed partnership can leave significant problems for subsequent leaders if things go wrong. Agreement on how to end arrangements is often as important as how to begin them.

New ways of working

Working with local PCT providers to run midwifery services within the children's centre is one example provided by one particular setting. The collaborative partnership has worked well and good planning and the employment of para-professional staff has assisted the delivery of the service.

Partnership working will require innovation in how services are delivered. This example understates the complex negotiation and creative organisation that enabled agreement and allowed the mixing of para-professional and professional staff. Encouraging professional staff to contemplate and engage with working in new ways is challenging. Professions have developed working systems over time based on their experiences of what is best, usually influenced by the potential for things to go wrong if protocols are not followed. Leaders need to be clear about the enormity of what they may be asking colleagues from different professional disciplines to contemplate and to be aware of the personal needs of those individuals as people, as the following example shows:

Joint Ofsted accreditation of the Community Lodge so that a pre-school service could be achieved with the school being the employing body of the early years staff and the capital building owned by the children's centre.

Children's centre leaders need to be prepared to take a degree of calculated risk, opening dialogue in order to overcome challenges creatively. In this example, ways and means were found to enable a pre-school service to be established which would not otherwise have been possible. Again the example states simply what was achieved but this masks the negotiations between school, children's centre and local authority, all of which had specific issues that needed to be satisfied before agreement could be reached. This example shows what can be achieved positively when there is a shared understanding between local authorities and schools with children's centres on site.

 Points for reflection

How can understanding of children's centres in local authorities be improved?

How can parents become confident contributors?

How far can children's centres be facilitators in the process of change?

What are the implications for leadership?

 Summary

This chapter has considered issues arising from change and the need to balance the differing agendas at national, local and centre levels. Balance is also required in terms of the tension between the need for stability and the need for change and creative innovation in ECEC services.

The key points to remember from this chapter are:

- understanding the importance of informed partnership with local authorities which can be a first step towards reviewing procedures and protocols which otherwise constrain and limit practice;

- understanding the differences and similarities between children's centres and schools, including the potential similarities and differences of children's centre and extended schools agendas;

- recognition of the value of and need for openness in approaching shared understandings between partner agencies at all levels;

- the importance of developing leadership skills in the Early Years, including a range of available leadership styles;

- the need to consider all partners and foster equal partnership between settings and children, parents and the community;

- the critical importance of clear communication if service users are to be fully included in identifying needs alongside the partner agencies that provide core services.

Further reading

For practice based examples of partnership working with parents:

- Draper, L. and Duffy, B. (2007) 'Working with parents', in G. Pugh and B. Duffy (eds), *Contemporary Issues in the Early Years*, 4th edn. London: SAGE, Chapter 11.

- Whalley, M. and the Pen Green Centre Team (2007) *Involving Parents in Their Children's Learning,* 2nd edn. London: Paul Chapman.

For Early Years leadership, including children's centres:

- Aubrey, C. (2007) *Leading and Managing in the Early Years.* London: SAGE.

For lessons learnt from Sure Start Local Programmes:

- Anning, A. and Ball, M. (eds) (2008) *Improving Services for Young Children: From Sure Start to Children's Centres.* London: SAGE.

Useful websites

The Children's Plan itself and the versions for parents and families and for young people are readily accessible online or in hard copy and provide a clear view of the government's priorities:

- www.dfes.gov.uk/publications/childrensplan/downloads

Department for Children, Schools and Families (2007) *The Children's Plan.* London: HMSO.

7

The 'new professionals'

This chapter looks more closely at what the new professional will need to look like in order to meet changing demands and emphases and how current training and development programmes match those needs to ensure high-quality engagement with all the groups shown in Figure 7.1. The chapter looks at the following:

- the context of the 'new professionals';
- the importance of practitioner research for the new professionals;
- what new skills the new professionals will need to meet these demands;
- the new job specification.

Introduction

This chapter presents a very personal view which is intended to provoke reflection and debate. In compiling it I have drawn on my own experience, information from colleagues and practitioners in the field and research literature, but what is presented is essentially one interpretation which I hope you will take issue with.

The context of the 'new professionals'

The context in which the new professionals are working remains heavily tied to traditional professional and commercial attitudes and practices which reflect the needs of the times in which they were created as individual and separate professions, but which are no longer adequate to meet developing needs. The hierarchy of perceived importance of professions and the pyramid of professional progression within them can generate attitudes and behaviour which can be major disabling factors to establishing effective partnership working. The new professionals have to balance the knowledge, skills and practices that their chosen professional identity trains them in with more open attitudes and dispositions focused on the skills, attitudes and dispositions that enable partnership working. The new professionals are pioneers, looking for ways and means to disassemble traditional forms of organisation and practice and reassemble them with others into new approaches and possibilities. It would be good to be able to develop skills and strengthen practice laterally as well as vertically. This would help to offset the pressure to use qualifications and the achievement of designated status, including EYPS, to strengthen the over-all management and leadership of Early Years, which is likely to be a dominant influence for some time to come.

Key features of the 'new professionals'

Key features of the new professionals involve values and principles. In his introduction to *The 7 Habits of Highly Effective People*, Stephen Covey (2004) makes his case for more principled approaches to the way we manage and live our lives. Under separate headings he explores eight of 'the most common challenges we face', advocating under 'body, mind, heart and spirit' a balanced healthy lifestyle, reading broadly and deeply and continuous education, deep, respectful listening and serving others, and recognising that the source of the positive things we seek lies in principles (Covey, 2004: 11). He also refers to the need for 'creative cooperation' in dealing with conflict and differences. Covey recognises that as individuals we are in a 'current context' and the principles we strive to attain may be in conflict with the pressures of life and the institutions which surround us. We need to have clarity of vision and values to under-pin and develop our confidence and well-being, which in turn generates the courage to live what we believe and challenge the things that prevent this.

Daniel Goleman (1999) has developed the concept of emotional intelligence and sets out five elements which form its basis: self-awareness, motivation, self-regulation, empathy and adeptness in relationships. He links this to the concept of emotional competence, which he defines as 'how much of that potential we have translated into on the job capabilities' (Goleman, 1999: 24). It is skill in emotional competence which determines how successfully we can challenge in a respectful, positive manner which will open and enable discussion rather than close it.

Mark Friedman (2005) explores the field of performance measures and suggests more fair and realistic ways of designing and reporting performance measures in public services. A key concept is the idea of 'turning the curve' (Friedman, 2005: 58) which allows more credit for movements towards success, rather than a straight success/fail judgement. Accountability is increasingly important, not as a means of penalising providers or catching them out, but as the means of celebrating their successes. In order to achieve this the new professionals at the point of service delivery will need to be more aware of challenging inappropriate evaluation meth-ods by positively suggesting more appropriate alternatives: those in the planning and accounting phases will also need to be more aware of alternatives and be open to suggestions for further improvements. This can only be achieved through good communication and a commitment to more cooperative dialogue at each stage in conceptualising, planning, delivering and evaluating the services continuum.

Finally it is important not to lose sight of Bronfenbrenner's (1996) ecological sys-tems, which place the child at the heart of important influences centred on the family. Bronfenbrenner argues that the interaction between child and people, places and objects around them is what shapes their development. He refers to the interaction as 'proximal processes' and these can include indirect effects such as the laws which govern the community and parents' working conditions.

The new professionals, then, will need to embody attributes and attitudes which are more principled and sensitive, more considerate and reflective, better grounded in knowledge of current developments and research, more creative in responding to challenges, better able to evaluate, more adaptable and more open to redesign in response to changing needs. If this sounds too woolly or 'touchy feely' it is as well to remember that they will also have to be focused in their areas of expertise and practice, assertive in acquiring the resources to provide the services they have helped identify and credible in accounting for the value and effectiveness of those services. It is far easier and more comfortable to be told what to do and not to have to think or create than it is to actively participate as an equal voice in a 'flat hierarchy'. The new professionals will have to be able to manage discomfort, challenge and disequilibrium and use them positively to create new understandings.

The wider picture and its relevance

The need for all countries to invest in early education and care and to improve the workforce qualification levels and status are among the key findings from *Starting Strong II* (2006), an OECD report on 20 countries from the developed world. In the context of the needs of the Early Years workforce the report notes, inter alia, the following developments compared with an earlier review in 2001 (Bennett, 2003): a growing consensus that governments need to provide planned and regulated investment to develop early childhood education and care services to meet research-based evidence on demographic, social and cost-benefit changes. Developing more highly qualified Early Years professionals is another priority identified, as is the need for increased practitioner involvement with research. All of the key findings directly underscore the themes of this chapter. The details of this summary can be found at the OECD website (see Useful websites at the end of the chapter).

The importance of practitioner research for the new professionals

The emphasis on continuing professional development to improve the lives of children is promoted and reinforced in the UK by the Children's Workforce Development Council (CWDC). Their website includes separate sections on professional development and integrated working as well as details of apprenticeships and other relevant qualifications (www.cwdcouncil.org.uk/integrated-working). A clear implication in addition is that the new professionals will engage in practitioner research. The value and importance of research as a means of monitoring and evaluating existing practice, and of informing future planning, is emphasised by the OECD (2006) report. While this mainly refers to the strategic level it is also true of each level and practitioner research has an important part to play. The new professionals will need sound knowledge of developing social and educational theory and in practice. They will need to be aware of the lessons learnt in the past but be open to change and willing to innovate as well. They will have to be able to work with colleagues from other professions and prepared to approach issues in an open-minded and developmental way. They will have to be comfortable with initial uncertainty and constant adjustment. They will have to be aware of their own and the wider picture. They will need to be well supported, mentored and have good opportunities for ongoing training and development.

Throughout Europe and further afield, early childhood research has been strongly influenced by social pedagogy, exploring the links between ECEC and the social context of the country in which the children are growing up. Social pedagogy focuses on association, groups, community and related interactive processes. The growing awareness of associated influences and issues has helped to develop heightened awareness and changing policies and approaches. Reggio Emilia is a good example of this. Conference themes in the UK and across Europe increasingly reflect social pedagogy and practitioner research and the sharing of findings and debate over the philosophy, aims and practice underpinning approaches to ECEC has developed significantly over the last decade. The European Early Childhood Education Research Association (EECERA) is an organisation which has attracted worldwide support from researchers in Early Years care and education and proved a lively theatre for debate and information sharing, working in partnership with host countries. Early childhood literature has reflected the groundswell gathering momentum and shape. For example, the autumn 2008 edition of *Children in Europe* magazine included an article by Professor Jan Peeters from Ghent University pointing to the need for new professionals to match the new demands arising from the changes in understanding and approach to Early Years care and education. Professor Peeters is exploring the implications of changing circumstances for the Early Years workforce across Europe and in his book published in 2008, *The Construction of a New Profession: A European Perspective on Professionalism in Early Childhood Education and Care*, which included an article based on his academic research, Peeters calls for the international co-construction of a 'democratic professionalism in early childhood education and care'.

 Activity

Visit the OECD Starting Strong II website (see Useful websites at the end of the chapter) and compare findings from any two countries.

Reflect on what you find in terms of similarities and differences in their practices.

Partnership working aims revisited

Figure 7.1 shows the groups which surround the child and are focused on identifying and meeting the child's needs. They are the groups at the heart of the Every Child Matters agenda. Each group is a complex structure and its members have their own dynamics and needs. Synthesising the interaction of groups with each other, and the individual members themselves, into coherent partnership teams is extremely demanding and complex. All the organisations involved aim to address the following aspects but from different perspectives.

Identify and respond to the needs of children, families and communities

The statutory, private and voluntary agencies only exist to support children, families and communities. Local authority departments, Health, Social Services, Community Development, Connexions, Jobcentre Plus and agencies supporting debt avoidance and domestic financial management have all moved towards greater links with service users so that services are better matched to needs. There is still a great deal to be achieved in

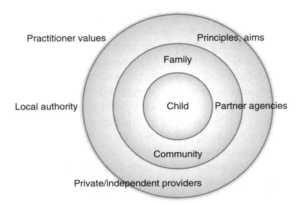

Figure 7.1   The child at the centre

terms of inter-agency coordination and cooperation and children's centres are seen by the government as having a key role. The best practice shows what can be achieved but there are still many examples where agencies are unaware of children's centres or what their role and function can include. The 'silo mentality' is hard to break.

Take account of the needs of the whole family

While Social Services are primarily focused on the care and welfare needs of the child, health visitors are similarly focused but in terms of physical development and growth, Education has a specific focus for children and parents, and services such as housing and drug and alcohol abuse counselling affect the whole family. There is a growing understanding of the value of working together to avoid scenarios where a course of action adopted by one agency inadvertently undermines that of another.

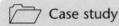 Case study

A family in crisis

Family A – mother, father and three children aged 4, 2 and 6 months. A family in crisis: father (30) drinks heavily and when he does so becomes violent towards mother; mother (21) is being treated for depression and obesity; parents on the verge of separating. Children – the 4-year-old, Sasha, has a place at nursery but attendance is erratic and when she attends she is solitary and unhappy. She has 'glue ear' but has not attended hospital appointments. The 2-year-old boy, Sean, is being monitored by the health visitor, who has recently reported bruising to Social Services. Sean has attended a 'stay and play' session with his mother at sessions run by children's centre staff at a community hall nearby. The baby, Susan, when monitored by the midwife, was found to have a low birth weight and since then the health visitor has recorded slow development.

In this example at this stage separate agencies might involve:

- Health – health visitor, hospital clinic, GP, possibly midwife, specialist input for depression and obesity;

- Community Mental Health;

- Social Services;

- Education – nursery leader, head teacher, secretary;

- Children's Centre – outreach worker, centre head.

Depending on the level of violence there may also be involvement of the police and refuge services. If each operates in isolation, with the best of intentions, it is conceivable that the family will be separated, with the possibility that the children will be taken into care. However, a more joined-up approach and a holistic view of family needs provide an opportunity to support each member to identify and address their own needs and their needs in relation to each other. In the context of this chapter, the point is that all professionals need to be open to and understand the possibilities of more joined-up working.

To do this requires open exchange of information and agencies can be very reluctant to do this for fear of infringing confidentiality. Why is it that the most intimate details can be shared at a case conference called by Social Services yet are deemed inappropriate for those same individuals to share outside such a meeting? The assumption seems to be that the individuals can only be trusted to observe confidence in a particular situation, even when to do so outside a formal meeting might enable professionals to support families concerned and avoid a worsening of the situation, which in turn would avoid the need for a case conference. Case conferences serve an important function and are still part of the multi-agency approach, but are often a blunt instrument: alternative intervention at earlier stages can support individuals and families and avoid the negative choices.

Bring services to the community rather than the reverse

The former approach of service providers was based in the expectation that people would come to them. This approach worked for those who were able to do so. It presupposes that people are not only aware of the services that exist but also of how to access them. It was also helped by knowledge and information staying relatively unchanged. This is no longer the case and change affects processes, locations and personnel, so information is outdated very quickly. The concerns over the high incidence of deprivation and poverty have provided research information which indicates the negative effects of poverty in reducing the well-being, confidence and stability of individuals, particularly mothers. This has been shown to have potentially negative effects on children and so to increase the cycle of deprivation (EPPE Reports 2004; DfES, 1997–2004; Child Poverty Action Group, (CPAG) 2008). The move to bring services to people combined with more effective consultation to identify the real concerns and needs together with a philosophy aiming to enable people to regain self-esteem and control of their lives is intended to break the cycle and redress the worst effects of poverty and deprivation.

Improve accessibility, particularly providing more open access to training and skills

Part of the process of change and breaking the cycle of poverty is to make more training and skill areas available to all. Parents now have access to programmes which aim to improve parent–child bonding, such as 'baby massage' and 'stay and play' where professionals work alongside groups of parents and their children. Courses on healthy eating, first aid and health and safety in the home help parents gain confidence and encourage healthier lifestyles. There are courses in IT and basic life skills which enable parents to improve their employability as well as raising confidence and self-esteem. The hidden benefits include encouraging those living more isolated lives to get out and gradually begin to be more confident in meeting others, and enables many to see that their concerns are not unique but are shared and in many ways 'normal' challenges. Opportunities can also be created for working parents, fathers and mothers to spend quality time with their children, engaged in activities organised and structured by skilled professionals who can model good practice where necessary. Parents who are confident are better placed to support and encourage their children. The services can include financial and budgeting advice.

Identify and reach the 'hard to reach'

Taking services to people and improving access can still miss many in society who for cultural, economic or social reasons remain isolated and unwilling or unable to engage. There are different reasons for some individuals and groups being 'hard to reach', not least those who actively avoid any kind of recognition or engagement. The belief is that there are still those who could benefit from services and whose views are important but who are not yet aware of what is possible.

 Points for reflection

How far do you share these partnership aims?

Do they meet the needs of children, families and communities?

How far has your training prepared you for these approaches?

Partnership working person specification: what are the key values, aims, principles, skills and qualities?

To begin to address the aims, individual practitioners need the existing skills they have been trained in and have learnt through practice in each of their professions, but need to use them in different ways, in effect helping systems and approaches to be developed that will meet the new demands. The new professionals will need to be more focused on addressing causes rather than effects wherever possible. The emphasis on practice that encourages parents, families and communities to take more control of their own lives and supports them in developing confidence and raising their self-esteem (cf. Every Child Matters, Children Act 2004) is fundamental to achieving long-term benefits. The skills required for building towards independence and empowering individuals, rather than reinforcing dependency, exist in some professions and among some professionals, but these skills need to be more fully understood by all and developed by a wider range of professions and agencies. Trust is a key aspect: establishing, fostering and maintaining trust with individuals and groups has always been an essential skill; applying this skill with individuals facing more challenging situations and being able to engage with them in a non-judgemental, supportive fashion in situations with which the key person themself is not fully familiar requires working with other colleagues and agencies fully while maintaining the integrity of that trust. Those working as a key person will require new or refreshed skill areas such as advocacy to provide a voice for vulnerable individuals and groups and will depend on the quality of that trust. In addition all professionals will increasingly have to be prepared, in the sense of being trained, to be able to make hard choices wisely in order to ensure the highest priority is given to the area of greatest need, with the child at the centre. While in the past this may have been a senior decision, increasingly practitioners will face choices of these kinds in their daily practice. In order to have the confidence to assess situations and decide priority and appropriate action, they will need specific training and an awareness of where their colleagues in other professional agencies fit into the specific case as well as the wider picture.

In order for practitioners to be aware of these principles and develop the skills they will need to put them into practice, they need to have a leadership which is committed to encouraging their own well-being and self-awareness. Encouraging an improved awareness of their personal professional skills, deepening their self-understanding and encouraging honesty with themselves is part of the developing process to enable staff to encourage similar feelings in those they support. Leaders themselves are in an area that is changing and where there is a need to assess situations and create services and systems to meet the assessed needs often using innovative approaches. The essence of ECEC services is to identify new or unmet needs and to work with those who have not been able to access services previously as well as those who have. If staff are to be supported they will need new approaches too, such as the 'flat hierarchies' mentioned in Chapter 6, teamwork where the 'team' will be multi-professional and may well be based on several sites, open mindedness where they are no longer the 'all-knowing professional', and approaches that are 'bottom-up' rather than 'top-down'.

 Activity

How has change affected you?

Can you recall and summarise an example of a leader who has inspired you?

What new skills will the new professionals need to meet these demands?

Expectations

The expectations are based in the knowledge that new professionals will be working in partnership and are clear for all to see from the ECM website which sets out a blueprint for the future (www.everychildmatters.gov.uk/aims/childrenstrusts/). There is a clear statement that to achieve effective working there will be joint training to meet diverse needs including cultural and professional differences. The lead professional model is suggested where groups cover several professions and there is an expectation of co-location in extended schools and in children's centres. A combination of central and local organisation and control will run processes such as the Common Assessment Framework and support for the children's trusts. Integrated delivery will be matched by integrated strategy to ensure the system as a whole meets children's prioritised needs and will feature joint needs assessment, shared decisions on priorities, resource identification and joint planning to deploy those resources. The intention of this joint commissioning, underpinned by pooled resources, will ensure that those best able to provide the right packages of services can do so. All of this requires arrangements for governance that ensures everyone shares the vision and gives each the confidence to relinquish day-to-day control of decisions and resources while maintaining the necessary high-level accountability for meeting their statutory duties in a new way. New ways of sharing information using online services or a combination of telephone and keyboard so that information is more accessible and can reach a wider range of people are gradually emerging. But systems alone will not solve the issues – only the people themselves can do that.

Unifying features

Across the whole system there are some unifying features which help to link the various elements. Children's trusts are a valuable component in the process of identifying and meeting needs. Leadership has been recognised as key at every level and the emerging training programmes (NPQICL, EYFS) are intended to begin to address this need. The coordinating ECM website also lists 'performance management' outcomes, focuses and reward incentives. This is more problematic in that any lack of the kind of skills expected of practitioners on the part of those setting performance targets and measuring progress could prove a major disincentive. However, there is an emphasis on listening, and this has clearly been the case in the way the Children's Plan has been devised. Hopefully the listening will also extend to practitioners and leaders. While there is much that is new and exciting there are echoes of the past and a risk of constraining initiative within a framework which may appear initially loose but tightens with use.

This underscores the need for the fundamental attitudes and attributes associated with principled practice and is further reinforced by the Key Elements of Effective Practice (KEEP – available on the teachernet website at www.teachernet.gov.uk/teachingandlearning/EYFS/abouteyfs/KEEP) identified by the DCSF Standards. These reflect the values, attributes, skills and principles already suggested:

> Effective practice in the early years requires committed, enthusiastic and reflective practitioners with a breadth and depth of knowledge, skills and understanding. Effective practitioners use their own learning to improve their work with young children and their families in ways which are sensitive, positive and non-judgmental.

> (http://nationalstrategies.standards.dcsf.gov.uk/node/84399)

KEEP goes on to suggest the following list of skills for practitioners to develop and improve:

- focusing on relationships;

- understanding children's learning styles and varying development needs and linking these to children's interests;

- the knowledge and understanding required to support and extend children's learning;

- working with parents, carers, the wider community; and

- working with other professionals 'within and beyond the setting'.

The expectation of partnership working is explicit and will require specific skills from all who are working children and families, reflecting the same emphasis shown elsewhere.

The Early Year's Foundation Stage (EYFS) has a set of Principles into Practice cards setting out the four EYFS themes. These carry links to Other National Standards pages, to teachernet and to Ofsted which include access to evaluation tools for local authorities, illustrating the key elements of Early Years expertise required to implement the principles for Early Years care and education.

 Activity

Go to the ECM website: www.everychildmatters.gov.uk/aims/childrenstrusts/.

What more can you find to clarify what the trusts are and how they work?

The new job specification

What might a person specification for anyone engaging in partnership working include? What key attributes, attitudes and principles would they need to possess? Figure 7.2 is a person specification from an actual job specification for a children's centre services manager.

The specification sets clear qualification parameters from a wide base, accessible to a range of professional heritages, including qualification by experience. The 'special knowledge' includes practical management and leadership experience but also experience of interagency and community working, Early Years and multicultural issues. The inclusion of 'family-centred value base' in personal qualities and the range of positive qualities gives a clear message. In many respects the emphases in the document reflect the issues raised in Chapter 5 in terms of the local authority role and perspective and illustrate the natural priorities. But alongside the clear emphasis on practical skills needed to begin to carry out the role appear additional motivational attributes, listening skills, enthusiasm and creativity. There is no doubt of the administrative expectations but there is also a clear message in terms of the required process and enabling skills. The reality is that there is a wide range of attributes and skills which any children's centre service manager or centre manager will need to develop which are not apparent from the specification. Some of these may appear contradictory, for example balancing focus on process and outcomes equally when the expectation is clearly more outcomes orientated. While there is clearly a long way to go in including process attributes in more detail as an integral part of the job specification, there are indications of a shift which begins to recognise some of the process aspects.

Factors	Essential	Desirable	Measured by
Qualifications and skills			
• Educated to degree level	✓		
• Professional qualification in teaching, social care, welfare, health or associated areas *or* proven in-depth experience from working in a people orientated service	✓		
• Qualification in management		✓	
Special knowledge, abilities and/or experience			
• Minimum three years post-qualification experience in a similar role or environment	✓		
• Experience of managing a team in a complex environment	✓		
• Management experience, including budgets	✓		
• Experienced in leading and motivating a team		✓	
• Knowledge and experience of inter-agency structures	✓		
• Experience of project management supporting the development of new initiatives	✓		
• Experience of working with the local community	✓		
• Experience of the practical application of legislation relating to children and families			
• Commitment to non-discriminatory and anti-oppressive practice		✓	
• Early Years Development – knowledge of multicultural issues		✓	
• Knowledge of local area and local partnerships	✓		
• Experience of monitoring and evaluation processes	✓		
• Ability to communicate in writing and verbally, with professional individuals and groups in a manner that is clear and non-patronising	✓		
• Ability to prioritise work and meet deadlines			
• Ability to set clear objectives and lead a staff group in meeting these objectives	✓		
• Ability to manage relations with the media		✓	
• Ability to both give and receive high-quality supervision	✓		
• Good ICT skills		✓	
Personal qualities			
• Positive and facilitative	✓		
• Good listener, with ability to provide accurate feedback	✓		
• Enthusiastic and creative	✓		
• Family-centred value base	✓		
• Excellent interpersonal skills	✓		
• Able to respond to constructive criticism	✓		
• Flexibility to work evenings and weekends where necessary	✓		
• Driving licence	✓		

Figure 7.2 Job Specification – person specification for children's centre services manager
Reproduced with permission from North Warwickshire Early Years

ᘐᘐ Points for reflection

Compare this with your own or another job description: how does it match?

Where are the differences?

How might the missing aspects be developed?

Look at the job description in Figure 7.2 from the point of view of potential partners. How will each of the potential partners view the specification?

If you were on interview what would you believe the appointing panel would want to know?

Training and development programmes including NPQICL, NPQH and EYPS: How far does current training provide for these attributes, attitudes, knowledge and understanding?

Training for practitioners and leaders to meet the changing demands of child care and education agendas, linked with social change, has been a significant focus in government policy, under the remit of the Children's Workforce Development Council (CWDC). Early attempts to coordinate academic qualifications nationally and internationally in an equivalence structure proved complex and took longer than planned but have resulted in a more accessible system where qualifications can be accredited and transferred more easily. In leadership the National Qualification for Headteachers (NPQH) was established in education during the 1990s and has been further revised and developed by the National College for School Leadership (now known as 'The National College'). The National College are also responsible for the form, content and delivery of the training programme for leaders and managers in Early Years childcare and education, the National Professional Qualification in Integrated Centre Leadership (NPQICL). This provides an experiential, developmental programme centred on reflective practice which aims to encourage participants to explore value based practice and extend their knowledge and understanding of leadership and multi-agency working. Both of these qualifications aim to raise quality and standards.

While there are some similarities between the aims of these two senior leadership qualifications, there are also significant differences which become more acute where children's centres in England are located on school sites. Specific issues are discussed in Chapter 5; the focus here is implications for training leaders who will also be new professionals. The NPQICL is well established. The programme combines a focus on professional self-awareness with a framework of National Standards specific to leaders of partnership practice and adopts a process which provides direct experience of partnership working in the approach adopted to studying relevant skills and their theoretical grounding. In this way the process has equal importance to the outcome. A key feature is the development of reflective practice.

Some managers and leaders have also undertaken a Masters in Business Administration (MBA) qualification through university courses, to strengthen their knowledge of business organisation and practice. Many with the MBA qualification, while appreciating the management skills they have acquired, who have then undertaken NPQICL, have commented on how much more this focuses on leadership and multi-agency issues.

Qualifications for those involved in birth to 5 education and care have been increased and are promoted through the CWDC. The Council is one of six allied, partner agencies which constitute the 'Sector Skills Council for social care, children and young people's workforces in the UK'. The alliance partners are: Care Council for Wales, Children's Workforce Development Council, General Social Care Council, Northern Ireland Social Care Council, Scottish Social Services Council, and Skills for Care (www.skillsforcareanddevelopment.org.uk). The Skills for Care and Development (SfC&D) is licensed by government. The alliance is a multi-agency group working across all service providers relating to social care and development. It represents employers and work force involved in social care and education across the UK, from private and public organisations. Their role primarily includes working directly with service providers but also those who receive services where necessary. The emphasis is to support and develop:

> appropriately skilled and qualified workers to meet the UK's current and future social care needs.
>
> (www.skillsforcareanddevelopment.org.uk/view.aspx?id=15).

The Early Years Professional Status qualification is available through designated providers in England and aims to provide a comprehensive grounding in theory and practice relating to children's care and education from birth to 5 for those already working at different levels of qualification in Early Years. There are four different pathways into EYPS currently with another two in the process of development to increase its accessibility. The programme includes units focused on working with families, team work and collaboration including multi-agency working. EYPS is equivalent to Qualified Teacher Status (QTS) when completed and counts as 'practical experience' for those applying for Level 6 qualifications. There is an emphasis on the leadership aspects, by maintaining current knowledge, modelling best practice by example, providing practical advice to other practitioners, coaching, group sessions, planning and reflecting on practice, which reflect some of the themes in the NPQH and NPQICL. (Full details are available on the CWDC website: www.cwdcouncil.org.uk/eyps.)

There is a clear aim to match the raising of standards to a programme which is accessible to the widest range of relevant entry qualifications. This is part of the planned government Child Workforce Strategy. However, EYPS is a mark of the achievement of a 'status' and not a qualification as such. The difference is that although it mirrors the additional skilled teacher status points available to qualified and practising teachers who fulfil criteria for subject-based areas, the status does not carry any statutory additional payment for those who achieve it. The CWDC recommends a 'salary premium' should be paid in recognition of the impact that EYPS status holders will have and this may affect the way in which practitioners in ECEC and wider partner agencies perceive and value the status designation. Anecdotal evidence suggests that some private providers are reluctant to pay the premium or release the practitioners to disseminate good practice to competitors.

A local authority advisor who recently completed EYPS by the three-month validations provided the following comments:

> The process allowed me to ...
>
> - fulfil my personal development through gaining a further relevant qualification;
> - reflect on my leadership qualities and identify gaps for further professional development/experience;
> - focus on the 'enhancement' aspects of my job;
> - have an impact on my leadership role – self-reflective tool;
> - be part of a reflective learning community.
>
> And the cons ...
>
> - the relationship of EYP status with other roles within the Early Years sector;
> - perception of the role and how it is valued by others within and beyond the children's service workforce;
> - maintaining a voice for EYPs – where does it go from here?
>
> As an Early Years advisor I subscribe to the identified role of an EYP as outlined by the CWDC and wanted to experience the process for myself. On gaining the status I have maintained my involvement by mentoring other EYP candidates and by facilitating the local authority EYP network.

Although it is hard to see how the emphasis on increasing professional qualifications will increase the value of ECEC staff if this is not recognised financially, it is clear that from a practitioner's viewpoint there is genuine value and worth, even though there are some key questions remaining to be answered. The CWDC website, and the materials produced by the trainers all emphasise the raising of standards and improvement in quality. Links are included in the Useful websites section the end of this chapter.

 Points for reflection

What gaps do you see between training so far in place and the needs of practitioners?

How might these be met?

The EYPS content includes study units covering key areas of birth to 5 education and care, focused on the Early Years Foundation Stage. It is primarily child-centred but also includes working with parents and multi-agency working. To match the needs of the largely attitudinal person specification, the most important aspect is more to do with how it is delivered than what it is designed to cover. The process of EYPS learning and teaching will have a strong influence on the practice of those who attain it. The clear intention by setting the high standard of entry, with an emphasis on experience, is to scaffold the existing skills and learning and further develop them. However, the style of learning has a critical impact on the style adopted by participants when they return to the workplace. Didactic methods can easily, and sometimes inadvertently, become a model for practice processes.

This emphasis on process is deeply embedded in the NPQICL, where individual participants are introduced to the practicalities and challenges of teamwork through the programme structure. It is potentially part of the other qualifications but depends entirely on the style adopted by the institutions and staff responsible for programme delivery. While content is important, making a real and lasting difference to enabling the attitudes and dispositions identified in the person specification, those undertaking EYPS need to be nurtured into identifying their values and principles and how these underpin their practice. An equally important, unresolved issue is the value those inside and outside the profession place on EYPS. Currently there is no professional body to represent them. Although the intention was for the EYPS status to be equal to QTS, in practice the lead roles in Early Years are being given to those holding the latter qualification. Pay differentials represent another contentious area: EYPS pay is subject to market forces whereas those with QTS have a standardised pay scale (Miller, 2008). While these factors remain unresolved they present significant toxins to the values, attitudes and attributes that underpin enabling partnership working and the motivation and self-worth of those holding the new qualifications.

Conclusion

What is the match between training, person specification and research? The person specification and findings from anecdotal evidence mirror skills and needs identified by a wide range of researchers and writers including Anning et al. (2006), Nurse (2007) and Weinstein et al. (2003). I am suggesting that the identified characteristics apply to all involved in partnership working at whatever level and from whatever perspective. Partnership working is increasingly an expectation in the UK and across the developed world. In England the Common Assessment Framework (CAF) created to safeguard children by identifying and addressing the needs of children and families can only work effectively if partnership working is in place. The Extended Schools initiative also has a better chance of working well where those involved share the skills, attitudes and practice outlined above. In Wales schools now follow the New Foundation Stage which was put in place during 2008 and recognise the need to raise the quality and coverage of the pre-school stage, with greater coordination between the two. In Wales Sure Start has been established since 2003 and has an important part to play in moving the Early Years care and education agenda forward. In Scotland there has been a more measured and considered approach with extensive background research and consultation and Northern Ireland is taking a similar long-term view. In each case, however, partnership working is now a clear expectation. The creation of new bodies such as the CWDC is evidence of the government's commitment to match the agenda set out in Every Child Matters and meet the needs identified for a more skilled and better trained Early Years workforce. The increased availability of training at different levels is beginning to have an impact although the long-term value has yet to be assessed. There does remain, however, the question of the extent to which the training and qualifications assist practitioners in meeting the new professionals' person specification and how all of this will work to meet the needs of children and families in practice.

 Points for reflection

Are the expectations of the new professionals realistic and what will help or hinder them?

Summary

The key points to remember from this chapter are as follows:

- The demands of ECEC are changing and require new attitudes and approaches from staff, leaders, local authorities and government. These changes are influenced by the move towards systems where partnership working is a strong and fundamental element.

- Effective practice in the early years requires committed, enthusiastic and reflective practitioners with a breadth and depth of knowledge, skills and understanding who are able to adapt and respond positively to changing situations and needs.

- Effective practitioners use their own learning to improve their work with young children and their families in ways which are sensitive, positive and non-judgemental.

- The need for new and different skills is recognised by the government which is sponsoring training to equip professionals for new systems. The training programmes are in place for leaders and practitioners to begin to address the changing needs. The processes encouraged are as important as the content or outcomes.

- Research shows that the changes are shared across Europe and the developed world and that calls for partnerships to engage with identifying needs are being made.

- Attitudes are changing but there are still many examples of individual or corporate attitudes which have yet to match changing needs.

Further reading

- Barr, H., Koppel, I., Reeves, S., Hammick, M. and Freeth, D. (2005) *Effective Interprofessional Education: Development, Delivery & Evaluation*. Oxford: Blackwell/CAIPE, pp. 107ff.

- Bronfenbrenner, U. (1996) *The Ecology of Human Development*. London: Harvard University Press.

- Chandler, T. (2007) 'Working in multidisciplinary teams', in G. Pugh and B. Duffy (eds), *Contemporary Issues in the Early Years*, 4th edn. London: SAGE, Chapter 10, p. 135.

- Professor Jan Peeters' article can be found in the autumn 2008 edition of *Children in Europe* magazine.

Useful websites

- Read more of Bronfenbrenner's ecology at: www.mentalhelp.net/poc/view_doc.php?type= doc&id=7930&cn=28

For more information on the UK the following web page is useful: www.childreninscotland. org.uk/workforce

Further information on qualifications can be gained from the following websites:

- EYPS: www.cwdcouncil.org.uk/eyps/what-is-an-eyp

Accredited EYPS providers are listed at: www.cwdcouncil.org.uk/eyps/eyp-training-provider-details

NPQICL: www.ncsl.org.uk/npqicl-index

NPQH: www.ncsl.org.uk/programmes-index/npqh-index.htm

For more information and details of the OECD Starting Strong reports visit: www.oecd.org/ document/61/0,3343,en_2649_39263231_37426685_1_1_1_1,00.html

For information on social pedagogy visit: www.infed.org/socialpedagogy/

Other European sites include: www.childrenineurope.org

For more information about the European Early Childhood Research Association visit: www. eecera.org/

Conclusion

In compiling this book I have tried to remain faithful to the evidence provided by colleagues in the field, research and my own experience. I have to acknowledge that in writing about an area that I believe so passionately in there is a danger that my own predisposition will have influenced how the book is presented. It would be wrong to deny this or my own values but I hope that what has been presented here is accessible and provides a degree of balance. In this conclusion there are three aspects of multi-agency working I wish to stress:

- the necessity of multi-agency working;

- the complexity of multi-agency working;

- the future of multi-agency working.

The necessity of multi-agency working

The consequences of practice which works in isolation, sometimes expressed as a 'silo mentality', can be dreadful. More than one tragedy has been shown to be the direct result of failures of professionals to communicate and to take responsibility for seeing through concerns raised by one or more person or agency. All agencies responded in unison following Lord Laming's report into the death of Victoria Climbié and there was a surge in the momentum to work more closely together across agencies and professions. The Common Assessment Framework has been the outcome, but even that has not prevented continuing tragedies such as the case of Baby 'P' in 2007.

The examples provided in this book show what can be achieved at a local level when professionals and agencies work together with children, parents and communities. In many ways what is advocated is common sense and there are many examples from different aspects of life that show the need for and value of partnership working, from designing and constructing a house to the chain of connections which enables shops to provide fresh food and produce. In these cases different groups and individuals use specific skills to contribute to a known end. The difference in the case of partnership working in the Early Years is that the end is known only in principle: to enable children to develop and thrive physically, intellectually, socially and spiritually. However, the precise nature of the 'end' is not known and in some ways never ends but continues to develop as individuals grow in understanding and knowledge in the spirit and practice of 'lifelong learning'. The consequences of not getting it right in the case of our children are serious but are often far less obvious, unless you happen to know the individual concerned or be directly involved in some way.

We can and must 'get it right'. For the sake of future generations we cannot afford to lose the potential of a single child. We need the separate skills of the different parts of the Health sector, Social Care and support, Education and Community Development to enable children, parents, families and communities to reduce dependency and to achieve their potential. Experience shows this is better achieved in partnership than in isolation. This does not mean we all have to be the same: the richness in partnership working comes from the diversity of the partners and their special and unique perspectives. Sharing, listening, valuing and respecting each other's points of view has been shown to produce innovation and more effective ways to meet individual and local needs, as well as enabling nationally identified areas to be addressed.

The complexity of multi-agency working

It is important not to underestimate the complexity of multi-agency working. Table 4.1 in Chapter 4 illustrates the wide range of partners and Chapter 5 shows how each of these may be at different stages of partnership in different settings and locations.

One of the issues affecting the development of partnership working in the Early Years and wider arenas such as the Common Assessment Framework is that new ideas are not created in isolation: they have a history which involves systems of organisation and practice and relationships between groups and individuals and at a personal level. These add to the complexity and need to be uncovered and acknowledged before they can be dealt with or there is a danger that they will fester and undermine the new and developing partnerships. Sanders, in Maynard and Thomas (2008: 186ff.), emphasises the need to consider the degree of integration of multidisciplinary teams and groups as well as the professional mix and the roles individuals have within and outside the teams. Understanding this complexity and developing strategies to lead and manage such diverse groups indicates a need for specifically skilled, trained and visionary leaders.

The current training programmes for leaders begin to address these areas but need to be further developed and extended. Training for those aspiring to leadership also needs to take into consideration raising the awareness of the complexity of and the different strategies for dealing with the implications of multi-agency practice. Not least among the skills are those involved in supervision. This aspect of professional practice is understood and welcomed by some professions but is not part of the culture and practice of others, particularly Education. It illustrates another feature of the complexity: that similar phrases and terms can mean utterly different things to different professions and to parents.

Yet the complexity can be used productively and positive attitudes can be engendered and used to move forward, even when individuals may share uncertainty about the final shape or pattern of a service or the means to achieve it. This brings us comes back to visionary leadership. Without positive leadership, which can see possibilities and entertain new ways forward, partnership working is at best limited, at worst doomed.

The example of what can be achieved when there is the political will, combined with a systematic approach grounded in research which takes account of the views of all partners, is clear to see in the way in which New Zealand approached Te Whaariki. This stands as an example at local, national, and international levels.

The future of multi-agency working

It is clear that it is very hard, if not impossible, for multi-agency working to succeed without the agreement and good will of those involved. The current emphasis nationally and within some professions on exploring and developing partnerships is a valuable foundation for progress. It is the beginning of national leadership in this direction.

What is essential is that coherent leadership is established at each level: national, regional, local and setting. Currently this is not the case: while there is developing leadership at setting level and within some local areas, there is no single body with overall control. The future of partnership working in Early Years and other areas depends on much clearer leadership, with actual authority and responsibility to promote, develop and oversee partnership working. Leadership of this sort is needed to address misunderstanding, reluctance and distrust where it exists and to identify and support good practice. It is also needed to set the standards which exist currently, but also to show how they can be attained.

In conjunction with appropriate and enabling leadership there also needs to be adequate funding. In each of the programmes which laid the foundations for children's centres, there was significant progress when funding was at its initial peak. Once the word 'sustainable' appeared service provision became compromised and choices had to be made about what to continue to support and what to cut. If lasting change is to be achieved, funding needs to be secured for the longer term. Sustainability is important and must be achieved, but when it is used to mean 'learn how to manage the same level of provision here on less funding', there is a danger that it becomes a weasel term and undermines confidence rather than stimulating challenge.

Funding overlaps with issues of staffing and terms and conditions of employment. The emphasis on raising quality by providing a more highly qualified workforce does allow for an improvement, but only if those achieving new qualifications also have a reasonable financial expectation. Valuing the contribution of Early Years staff has to include 'value' in all its senses. There are still issues over terms and conditions of employment that were highlighted in 2000 (Bertram et al., 2001), which have still not been addressed, other than within a few isolated examples of innovative practice. The merging of pre-school and school agendas through EYFS has underlined the need to identify and address the implications of the differences between care and education priorities and, how these services are structured and run, in order to provide suitable terms and conditions for all staff operating within the whole EYFS range. In particular those involved in and responsible for school leadership and governance need to be helped towards a better understanding of the nature and purpose of children's centres and where practice is similar to and different from schools.

At all levels partnership working will benefit from the development of reflective practitioners who consider what they do and why and who are prepared to share ideas and debate issues and approaches to arrive at improved practice. This can be supported and developed by effective supervision and mentoring, either by line managers or by suitably qualified providers from within or outside an organisation. There are already too few good quality leaders and we cannot afford to lose any of them for the want of a 'critical friend' or a 'professional ear'.

A final reflection on partnership working

Some things need to be unravelled to be understood, to make sense.

Others cannot be disentangled, unravelled without being broken or fundamentally changed. Even if these are re-constructed they will never be as they were.

Some things need to be re-formed in order to change, develop, grow, to increase their capacity to fulfil their potential, achieve what they could be.

We need to be aware of this and alert enough to perceive what makes each one as it is. We must be sensitive to which we might be dealing with. If we work together, perhaps we have more chance of knowing which is which?

Useful websites and organisations

Papers

- http://image.guardian.co.uk/sys-files/Guardian/documents/2002/12/09/damilola.pdf (Report of the Inquiry by Sir John Stevens into the death of Damilola Taylor – accessed 9 July 2008)
- www.cpag.org.uk/info/Povertyarticles/Poverty129/wellbeing.htm (CPAG, Child Poverty and Governemnt Policy Overview, Winter 2008)
- www.everychildmatters.gov.uk/deliveringservices/caf/
- www.leeds.ac.uk/medicine/menu/lifelong07/papers
- www.ness.bbk.ac.uk/
- www.surestart.gov.uk/publications/?Document=1501 (Early Reports – The Quality of Early Learning, Play and Childcare Services in SSLPs, NESS, 2005)
- www.surestart.gov.uk/research/keyresearch/eppe/ (EPPE Project website link)
- www.swap.ac.uk/learning/IPE4.asp (Interprofessional education 1: Definition and drivers)
- www.teachernet.gov.uk/wholeschool/familyandcommunity/workingwith parents/everyparentmatters/
- www.york.ac.uk/depts/spsw/mrc/documents/QPB14.pdf (domestic violence – accessed January 2009)

International information

OECD, *Starting Strong II: Early Childhood Education and Care:*

- www.oecd.org/document/63/0,3343,fr_2649_39263231_37416703_1_1_1_1,00.html
- www.oecd.org/document/61/0,3343,en_2649_39263231_37426685_1_1_1_1,00.html (press release, accessed July 2006)
- Australia: www.oecd.org/dataoecd/16/48/37423214.pdf
- Denmark: www.oecd.org/dataoecd/16/42/37423394.pdf
- Finland: www.oecd.org/dataoecd/16/2/37423404.pdf
- Ireland: www.oecd.org/dataoecd/15/63/37423587.pdf
- Italy: www.oecd.org/dataoecd/15/62/37423597.pdf
- Norway: www.oecd.org/dataoecd/16/18/37423694.pdf
- Sweden: www.oecd.org/dataoecd/16/16/37423778.pdf

New Zealand:

- www.minedu.govt.nz/index.cfm?layout=document&documentid=6413&indexid=7689&indexparentid=10943

New Zealand Te Whaariki:

- www.minedu.govt.nz/index.cfm?layout=document&documentid=3567&data=l

  - Early Childhood Curriculum – Te Whariki
  - Providing Positive Guidance
  - Desirable Objectives and Practices
  - Quality in Action
  - EC Professional Development Agreements 2005–2006

- www.cyf.govt.nz/documents/BTC_StopAbuse.pdf

USA:

- www.highscope.org/Research/PerryProject/perrymain.htm
- www.evidencebasedprograms.org/Default.aspx?tabid=32 (Summary of Perry Preschool Project – High Scope)
- www.ncjrs.gov/pdffiles1/ojjdp/181725.pdf (US Department of Justice (2000) detailed description of High Scope/Perry Preschool Project in relation to juvenile crime in pdf format)
- www.unicef.org/publications/files/SOWC_2005_(English).pdf

UK information

- EPPE: www.ioe.ac.uk/schools/ecpe/eppe/ (accessed 9 July 2008)
- OECD: www.oecd.org/dataoecd/16/15/37423795.pdf (accessed July 2008)
- www.nmc-uk.org.uk/aArticle.aspx?ArticleID=2344 (accessed 19 October 2008)

Wales:

- www.publications.parliament.uk/pa/ld199798/ldhansrd/vo971119/text/71119-05.htm
- www.surestart.gov.uk/aboutsurestart/help/contacts/wales/ (accessed July 2008)
- www.early-years-nto.org.uk/keyskill_briefing_wales.pdf (accessed February 2009)

Scotland:

- www.surestart.gov.uk/aboutsurestart/help/contacts/scotland/ (accessed July 2008)
- www.scotland.gov.uk/Publications/2006/01/24120649/4 (accessed January 2009)
- www.ltscotland.org.uk/earlyyears/professionaldevelopment/events/LTSseminars/earlyintervention.asp (accessed January 2009)
- www.scotland.gov.uk/library5/education/msss.pdf (accessed July 2008)
- www.scotland.gov.uk/Publications/2007/01/17162004/2 (Growing Up in Scotland study – accessed December 2008)
- http://urbact.eu/document-library/virtual-files/childhood/united-kingdom/mapping-sure-start-scotland.html (accessed July 2008)

- www.scotland.gov.uk/Publications/2009/01/13095148/2 (The Early Years Framework, December 2008 – accessed January 2009)

Northern Ireland:

- www.surestart.gov.uk/aboutsurestart/help/contacts/northernireland/ (accessed July 2008)
- www.deni.gov.uk/extended_schools_-_revised_18-9-06.pdf (accessed February 2009)
- www.deni.gov.uk/consultationsummary-2.pdf (Pre-school Education Review Summary 2004 – accessed November 2008)
- www.wellnet-ni.com/about.php
- www.nationalliteracytrust.org.uk/familyreading/casestudies/Dunagiven. html
- www.northernchildcare.com/memberagencies.htm

England:

- NESS: www.ness.bbk.ac.uk/ (accessed January 2008)
- www.dcsf.gov.uk/everychidmatters/research/evaluations/nationalevaluation/latest reports/latestreports/
- The Children Act 2004 (c. 31): www.opsi.gov.uk/Acts/acts2004/ukpga_ 20040031_ en_1 (accessed November 2008)

The Children's Plan:

- www.dfes.gov.uk/publications/childrensplan/downloads/Childrens_ Plan_ Executive_Summary.pdf (accessed November 2008)
- www.dfes.gov.uk/publications/childrensplan/downloads/The_Childrens_ Plan.pdf (accessed November 2008)
- www.dfes.gov.uk/publications/childrensplan/downloads/Childrens_Plan_ Parents_Families.pdf (accessed November 2008)
- www.dfes.gov.uk/publications/childrensplan/downloads/The_Childrens_ Plan.pdf (Introduction by Ed Balls, Secretary of State for Children, Schools and Families – accessed November 2008)

Standards:

- Early Years Foundation Stage:
  - www.standards.dfes.gov.uk/eyfs/ (accessed February 2009)
  - www.standards.dcsf.gov.uk/eyfs/site/about/index.htm (accessed July 2008)

- Every Child Matters:
  - www.everychildmatters.gov.uk/aims/background/ (accessed July 2008)
  - www.everychildmatters.gov.uk/aims/childrenstrusts/ (accessed July 2008)
  - www.teachernet.gov.uk/_doc/11184/6937_DFES_Every_Parent_Matters_ FINAL_PDF_as_published_130307.pdf (accessed July 2008)
  - www.dcsf.gov.uk/everychidmatters/research/evaluations/latestreports
  - www.dcsf.gov.uk/everychildmatters/earlyyearssurestart/whatsurestartdoes

- Every Parent Matters:
  - www.everychildmatters.gov.uk/_files/C900369CA2BA5349952531C5D1F1A327.pdf

KEEP:

- Key Elements of Effective Practice (KEEP): www.11million.org.uk/ (Office of the Children's Commisioner – accessed November 2008)

Quality improvement

- Early Years Quality Improvement Support Programme (EYQISP):http://national strategies.standards.dcsf.gov.uk/node/126433
- http://nationalstrategies.standards.dcsf.gov.uk/search/results/%22Quality+Improvement %22

Children's centres – core offer

- www.standards.dfes.gov.uk/primary/faqs/foundation_stage/1162267/#1162313 (accessed December 2008)
- www.togetherforchildren.co.uk (accessed December 2008)
- www.childrens-centres.org/default.aspx (accessed January 2009) – Home page of the Children's Centres pages of togetherforchildren
- www.nottinghamshire.gov.uk/home/learningandwork/preschool/earlyyears education/eydcp.htm (accessed May 2008)
- www.n-somerset.gov.uk/Education/Early+years/Childrens+Centres/coreservices offeredbychildrenscentres.htm (accessed May 2008)
- www.oldham.gov.uk/living/every_child_matters/childrens_centres.htm (accessed May 2008)
- www.fatherhoodinstitute.org/index.php?id=3&cID=421 (accessed November 2008)
- http://publications.dcsf.gov.uk/eOrderingDownload/DCSF-RB083.pdf (accessed March 2009)

Training

- NPQICL: www.ncsl.org.uk/programmes-index/npqicl-index.htm (accessed August 2008)
- NPQH: www.ncsl.org.uk/programmes-index/npqh-index.htm (accessed August 2008)
- EYPS:
  - www.cwdcouncil.org.uk/EYPS (accessed November 2008)
  - www.bestpracticenet.co.uk/eyps (accessed December 2008)
  - www.cwdcouncil.org.uk/page404 (accessed December 2008)
  - www.cwdcouncil.org.uk/eyps/eyp-training-provider-details (accessed December 2008)

- www.worc.ac.uk/courses/6850.html (accessed October 2008)
- www.cwdcouncil.org.uk/eyps/what-is-an-eyp (accessed August 2008)

Integrated working

- www.gscc.org.uk/NR/rdonlyres/D2517B64-E968-43B3-83E7-CA8AED2D EB02/0/Keyattributes.pdf (*Values for integrated working with children and young people* – accessed October 2008)
- www.cwdcouncil.org.uk/integrated-working (accessed August 2008)
- www.camden.gov.uk/ccm/content/contacts/council-contacts/education-council-contacts/contact-the-early-years-intervention-team.en (accessed February 2009)

Glossary

Andragogy   This relates to the theory and practice of approaches to the learning and teaching of adults. It is also 'person centred' and takes account of issues concerning where individuals are starting from and includes emotional as well as cognitive or experiential factors affecting their abilities to learn.

Children's Centres   These were established to address the effects of poverty on child and adult development. The centres were initially established in areas of greatest deprivation and aimed to bring together Social, Health and Education services for children aged 0–4 and adults, to make them more readily accessible. A parallel aim was to empower children, parents and communities to contribute to the planning and delivery of services as equal partners. The government's aim is to have Children's Centres more widely established and universally available in all local authorities by 2010.

Comenius Programme   One of several education projects funded by the EU, in this case to encourage partnerships between schools and universities among member countries to engage in joint research and information-sharing projects.

Connexions   Information and advice centres in England for teenagers aged 13–19, also available online. It provides support for teenagers and young people with learning disabilities up to age 25.

Early Excellence Centres   This innovative programme was overseen by Margaret Hodge during her time as a Minister within the DfES. While smaller in scale and funding than Sure Start, the programme had a significant impact alongside Sure Start in shaping future programmes, particulalrly the children's centre programme. Unlike Sure Start the programme was based on a centre rather than an area, and included the significant aim of using sites as training bases for professional development and multi-agency development. An initial group of nine designated centres expanded over a three-year period to exceed 100 settings. Uniquely this was a developmental programme from the outset encouraging different models of organisation and partnerships. While taking account of need, the centres were not targetted solely at the highest levels of deprivation.

Mentor   Someone who is trained to listen and assist in reflection on issues affecting an individual's work and responsibilities. They usually have some knowledge of the context, although this is not necessarily so, and may be a colleague or someone outside the workplace. Mentors are used in business and in universities and schools to suppor students, children and teachers.

Paradigm   '(1) a typical example, pattern, or model of something. (2) a conceptual model underlying the theories and practice of a scientific subject. (3) *Gram.* a table of all the inflected forms of a word, serving as a model for other words of the same conjugation or declension' (*Oxford English Dictionary*). In this publication definition (2) is applicable.

Pedagogy   This relates to the theory and practice of approaches to children's learning and teaching. It usually infers approaches and understanding that are 'child centred' and which take account of child development.

Performance management   In this publication refers to the general monitoring of staff performance, including support, rather than disciplinary measures or protocols, which are concerned with competence procedures or appraisal.

Silo mentality   Describes the insular and narrowly focused approach which keeps agencies or individuals tied into their own perspectives and agendas and prevents them from engaging with perspectives other their own or those of their agencies or profession. In the context of this book it refers to a predominantly negative attitude and outlook to be overcome if multi-agency working is to succeed.

Supervision   In this publication refers to one-to-one support sessions usually provided by a line manager. The sessions normally last up to three hours and provide an opportunity to explore issues, both celebratory and problematic, test ideas and possible strategies. The tone is normally positive and reflective.

Sure Start and **Sure Start Local Programmes**   This major programme was designed by the Blair New Labour government to provide support for children and families living in areas of high deprivation. As the programme developed it expanded over three phases, with a gradual reduction in the total funding available centrally and the aim for centres to become 'sustainable'. The expansion enabled areas other than those of highest deprivation to provide better quality access to services and the ultimate aim was to provide access to Sure Start in every community they served in their 'reach' area. A key principle was the aim of working with families and communities in order to seek out their actual needs rather than imposing external services. They had equal representation on steering committees. Sure Start merged into the Children's Centre programme. Local Sure Start Programmes were on a smaller scale, often as an outreach 'spoke' from a central 'hub'.

References

Anning, A. and Ball, M. (eds) (2008) *Improving Services for Young Children: From Sure Start to Children's Centres*. London: Sage.

Anning, A., Cottrell, D., Frost, N., Green, J. and Robinson, R. (2006) *Developing Multiprofessional Teamwork for Integrated Children's Services: Research, Policy and Practice*. Maidenhead: McGraw Hill Education/Open University Press, pp. 102–109.

Anning, A., Stuart, J., Nicholls, M., Goldthorpe, J. and Morley, A. (2007) *Understanding Variations in Effectiveness amongst Sure Start Local Programmes: Final Report*. London: DfES.

Athey, C. (1990) *Extending Thought in Young Children: A Parent–Teacher Partnership*. London: Paul Chapman.

Aubrey, C. (2007) *Leading and Managing in the Early Years*. London: Sage.

Baldock, P., Fitzgerald, D. and Kay, J. (2005) *Understanding Early Years Policy*. London: Paul Chapman.

Ball, C. (1994) *Start Right: The Importence of Early Learning*. London: RSA.

Barnett, G., Sellman, D. and Thomas, J. (eds) (2005) *Interprofessional Working in Health and Social Care: Professional Perspectives*. Oxford: Palgrave Macmillan.

Barr, H. (2002) *Interprofessional Education Today, Yesterday and Tomorrow,* Centre for Health Sciences and Practice Occasional Paper No. 1. London: Learning and Teaching Support Network.

Barr, H., Koppel, I., Reeves, S., Hammick, M. and Freeth, D. (2005a) *Effective Interprofessional Education: Argument, Assumption and Evidence*. Oxford: Blackwell/CAIPE.

Barr, H., Koppel, I., Reeves, S., Hammick, M. and Freeth, D. (2005b) *Effective Interprofessional Education: Development, Delivery and Evaluation*. Oxford: Blackwell/CAIPE.

Belsky, J., Melhuish, E. and Leyland, A. (2005) *Variation in Sure Start Local Programmes' Effectiveness: Early Preliminary Findings*. Nottingham: DfES Publications.

Bennett, J. (2003) 'Starting Strong: the persistent division between care and education', *Journal of Early Childhood Research*, 1(1): 21–48.

Bertram, T. and Pascal, C. (2000) *Early Excellence Centre Pilot Programme Annual Evaluation Report 2000*, DfES Research Report No. 258. Norwich: HMSO.

Bertram, A., Pascal, C. and Saunders, M. (2006) *Baby Effective Early Learning*. Birmingham: Amber Publishing.

Bertram, T., Pascal, C., Gasper, M., Mould, C., Ramsden, F. and Saunders, M. (2001) *Research to Inform the Evaluation of the Early Excellence Centres Pilot Programme*, DfES Research Report No. 259. Nottingham: DfEE.

Bertram, T., Pascal, C., Bokhari, S., Gasper, M. and Holterman, S. (2002) *Early Excellence Centre Pilot Programme Second Evaluation Report 2000–2001,* DfES Research Report No. 361. Norwich: HMSO, p.40 Typology of network EECs; p.77, p.108.

Bertram, T., Pascal, C., Bokhari, S., Gasper, M., Holtermann, S., John, K. and Nelson, C. (2003) *Early Excellence Centre Pilot Programme Third Annual Evaluation Report 2001–2002*. London: DfES.

Brighouse, T. et al. (2007) 'We call for review of early years law', *Times Educational Supplement,* 30 November.

Bronfenbrenner, U. (1996) *The Ecology of Human Development.* London: Harvard University Press.

Bruce, T. and Meggitt, C. (1997) *Childcare and Education.* London: Hodder and Stoughton.

Bruce, T. and Meggitt, C. (2006) *An Introduction to Child Care and Education,* 2nd edn. London: Hodder Arnold.

CAIPE (1997) *Interprofessional Education: A Definition.* London: Centre for the Advancement of Interprofessional Education, p. 9, quoted by Barr, H., Koppel, I., Reeves, S., Hammick, M. and Freeth, D. (2005) *Effective Interprofessional Education: Argument, Assumption and Evidence.* Oxford: Blackwell/CAIPE, p. xvii.

Chandler, T. (2007) 'Working in multidisciplinary teams', in G. Pugh and B. Duffy (eds), *Contemporary Issues in the Early Years,* 4 edn. London: Sage.

Child Poverty Action Group (2008) 'Child poverty and well-being in the here and now', *Poverty,* 129: 11–14, at p. 12; online at: www.cpag.org.uk/info/Povertyarticles/Poverty129/Poverty129childwellbeing.pdf.

Clark, M. M. and Waller, T. (2007) *Early Childhood Education and Care: Policy and Practice.* London: Sage.

Colmer, K. (2008) 'Leading a learning organization: Australian early years centres as learning networks', *European Early Childhood Education Research,* 16(1): 107–15.

Covey, S. R. (2004) *The 7 Habits of Highly Effective People.* London: Simon & Schuster, pp. 7–12.

Csikszentmihalyi, M. (1995) *Living Well: The Psychology of Everyday Life.* London: Weidenfeld & Nicholson.

Cunningham-Burley, S., Jamieson, L., Morton, S., Adam, R. and McFarlane, V. (2002) *Mapping Sure Start Scotland.* London: HMSO.

Dahlberg, G., Moss, P. and Pence, A. (1999) *Beyond Quality in Early Childhood Education and Care: Postmodern Perspectives.* London: Falmer.

Department for Children, Schools and Families (2007) *The Children's Plan.* London: HMSO.

Department for Children, Schools and Families (2008) *Child Development in the First Three Sweeps of the Millennium Cohort Study.* A. Cullis and K. Hansen, Institute of Education, University of London, Research Report DCSF RW 077, Summary of Findings.

Department for Education and Employment (2000) *First Findings.* London: DfEE.

Department for Education and Employment (2001) *Final Report of the Working Group for the Development of the Strategic Plan for Early Childhood Education October 2001.* London: DfEE.

Department for Education and Employment/Qualifications and Curriculum Authority (2000) *Curriculum Guidance for the Foundation Stage.* London: HMSO.

Department for Education and Science (1990) *Starting with Quality: Report of the Committee of Inquiry into the Educational Experiences Offered to Three and Four Year Olds* (Rumbold Report). London: HMSO.

Department for Education and Science (2003a) *Every Child Matters,* CM 5860. London: TSO.

Department for Education and Science (2005) *Early Impacts of Sure Start for Children and Families,* Research Report NESS/2005/FR/013. London: HMSO.

Department for Education and Skills (1997–2004) *The Effective Provision of Pre-School Education (EPPE) Project: Final Report, A Longitudinal Study.* London: DfES, online at www.dcsf.gov.uk/everychildmatters/publications/0/1160/.

Department for Education and Skills (2002a) *Birth to Three Matters: A Framework to Support Children in Their Earliest Years.* London: HMSO.

Department for Education and Skills (2002b) *Early Excellence Centre Pilot Programme Second Evaluation Report 2000–2001*, Research Report No. 361. Norwich: HMSO.

Department for Education and Skills (2003b) *National Standards for Under 8s Daycare and Childminding.* London: HMSO; now available at: www.dcsf.gov.uk/everychild matters/publications/0/?i_Page=60&.

Department for Education and Skills (2003c) *The Children's Workforce Strategy*, Consultation Paper. DfES.

Department for Education and Skills (2003d) *The Impact of Parental Involvement, Parental Support and Family Education on Pupil Achievement and Adjustment: A Literature Review*, Research Report RR433. Nottingham: DfES Publications.

Department for Education and Skills (2004a) *Every Child Matters: Change for Children.* Nottingham. DfES Publications.

Department for Education and Skills (2004b) *Choice for Parents, the Best Start for Children: A Ten-year Strategy for Childcare.* London: HMSO; now available at: www.dcsf.gov.uk/everychildmatters/earlyyears/surestart/aboutsurestart/strategy/10yearstrategy/.

Department for Education and Skills (2004c) *Every Child Matters: Next Steps.* London: HMSO.

Department for Education and Skills (2005) *Ten Year Strategy for Childcare: Guidance for Local Authorities.* London: HMSO.

Department for Education and Skills (2005b) *Higher Standards, Better Schools for All.* Norwich: HMSO; available online at: www.dfes.gov.uk/ publications/schoolswhite paper/ (accessed July 2007).

Department for Education and Skills (2007a) *National Standards for Leaders of Sure Start Children's Centres.* Nottingham: DfES.

Department for Education and Skills (2007b) *Every Parent Matters.* London: HMSO.

Department for Education and Skills (2007c) *Understanding Variations in Effectiveness Amongst Sure Start Local Programmes: Final Report,* NESS/2007/SF/024. London: DfES.

Department of Health and Social Services (1986) *Working Together: A Guide to Arrangements for Inter-agency Co-operation for the Protection of Children from Abuse.* London: HMSO.

Department of Health, Home Office and Department for Education and Employment (1999) *Working Together to Safeguard and Promote the Welfare of Children: A Guide to Inter-agency Working to Safeguard and Promote the Welfare of Children.* London: HMSO.

Department of Health/Welsh Office (1997) *People Like Us – The Report of the Review of Safeguards for Children Living Away from Home* (Utting Report). London: HMSO.

Desforges, C. and Abouchaar, A. (2003) *The Impact of Parental Involvement, Parental Support and Family Education on Pupil Achievement and Adjustment. A Literature Review.* London: DfES.

Ebbeck, M. and Waniganayake, M. (2002: 28), cited in C. Aubrey (2007) *Leading and Managing in the Early Years.* London: Sage, p. 136.

Edgington, M. (2007) 'Early Years in crisis? Reflecting on the past ten years, hoping for the future', *Early Years Educator*, 9(4): 22–4.

Epstein, J. L. and Saunders, M. G. (2002) 'Family school and community partnerships', in P. Baldock, D. Fitzgerald and J. Kay (2005) *Understanding Early Years Policy.* London: Paul Chapman, p. 94.

Fitzgerald, D. and Kay, J. (2008) *Working Together in Children's Services.* London: Routledge.

Freeth, D., Hammick, M., Koppel, I., Reeves, S. and Barr, H. (2005) *A Critical Review of Evaluations of Interprofessional Education.* Oxford: Blackwell/CAIPE.

Freidman, M. (2005) *Trying Hard is Not Good Enough: How to Produce Measurable Improvements for Customers and Communities.* Oxford: Trafford Publishing.

Freire, P. (1972) *Pedagogy of the Oppressed.* London: Penguin.

Gardner, R. (2003) 'Working together to improve children's life chances: the challenge of inter-agency collaboration', in J. Weinstein, C. Whittington and T. Leiba (eds), *Collaboration in Social Practice*. London: Jessica Kingsley, pp. 137–160.

Goleman, D. (1999) *Working with Emotional Intelligence*. London: Bloomsbury, p. 98.

Handy, C. (1994) *The Empty Raincoat*. London: Hutchinson, p. 65.

Hargreaves, A. and Fink, D. (2006) *Sustainable Leadership*. San Francisco: Jossey-Bass.

Her Majesty's Government (2004) *The Children Act*. London: Office of Public Sector Information.

Hochschild, A. (1983) cited in A. Hargreaves and D. Fink (2006) *Sustainable Leadership*. San Francisco: Jossey-Bass, pp. 218ff.

Holterman, S. (1994) *Becoming a Breadwinner*. London: Daycare Trust, cited in T. Maynard and N. Thomas (eds) (2008) *An Introduction to Early Childhood Studies*. London: Sage, p. 166.

Houston, A. M. and Houston, D. (2006) *Evaluating Family Support and Outreach Across the Sure Start Children's Centre Locality Teams in Camden*. Camden Local Authority.

Kagan, S. L. and Hallmark, L. G. (2001) 'Cultivating leadership in early care and education', *Child Care Information*, 140: 7–10, cited in P. Baldock, D. Fitzgerald and J. Kay (2005) *Understanding Early Years Policy*. London: Paul Chapman, p. 86.

Kelly, A. (2004) 'Child health', cited in T. Maynard and N. Thomas (eds) (2008) *An Introduction to Early Childhood Studies*. London: Sage, p. 171.

Kinos, J. (2008) 'Professionalism – a breeding ground for struggle. The example of the Finnish day-care center', *European Early Childhood Education Research*, 16(2): 224–41.

Laming, H. (2003) *The Victoria Climbié Inquiry*. London: HMSO.

Lane, J. (2006) *Right from the Start*. Trowbridge: Focus FIRST.

Lymbrey, M., 'Collaborating for the social and health care of older people', in J. Weinstein, C. Whittington and T. Leiba (eds) (2003) *Collaboration in Social Practice*. London: Jessica Kingsley, pp. 219–38.

Malaguzzi, L. (1993) 'For an education based on relationships', *Young Children*, 49 (1) 9–12.

Martin-Korpi, B. (2005) *Early Childhood Education and Care in Sweden – A Universal Welfare Model, Learning with other Countries*, Policy Paper No. 4. London: Daycare Trust, cited in OECD (2006) *Starting Strong II: Early Childhood Education and Care*. Paris: OECD Publishing.

Maslow, A.H. (1943) 'A theory of human motivation', *Psychological Review*, 50 (4): 370–96.

Maynard, T. and Thomas, N. (eds) (2008) *An Introduction to Early Childhood Studies*. London: Sage.

Meade, A. and Cubrey, P. (1995) Thinking Children. Wellington: New Zealand: Council for Educational Research.

Miller, L. (2008) 'Developing professionalism within a regulatory framework in England: challenges and possibilities', *European Early Childhood Education Research*, 16 (2): 255–68.

National Evaluation of Sure Start Research Team (2005) *Early Impacts of Sure Start Local Programmes on Children and Families*, Report No. 13. London: Department for Education and Skills; available online at: www.surestart.gov.uk/doc/P0001867. pdf.

National Evaluation of Sure Start Research Team (2008)*The Impact of Sure Start Local Programmes on Three Year Olds and Their Families*, Research Report NESS/2008/FR/027; available online at: www.ness.bbk.ac.uk/documents/ activities/impact/41.pdf.

Nurse, A. D. (ed.) (2007) *The New Early Years Professional: Dilemmas and Debates*. Oxford: Routledge.

Nutbrown, C. (1994) *Threads of Thinking*. London: Paul Chapman.

Nutbrown, C. (ed.) (1996) *Children's Rights and Early Education*. London: Paul Chapman.

Ofsted (2006) *Extended Services in Schools and Children's Centres*, HMI 2609. p. 4.

Organisation for Economic Cooperation and Development (2001) *Starting Strong: Early Childhood Education and Care*. Paris: OECD.

Organisation for Economic Cooperation and Development (2006a) *Starting Strong II: Early Childhood Education and Care*. Paris: OECD Publishing, Chapter 10.

Organisation for Economic Cooperation and Development (2006b) *Starting Strong II: Early Childhood Education and Care*. Paris: OECD Publishing, Executive Summary – available at: oecd.org/dataoecd/30/8/37519079.pdf.

Organisation for Economic Cooperation and Development (2006c) *Starting Strong II: Early Childhood Education and Care*. Paris: OECD Publishing, Annexe E – Australia, pp. 265–73.

Organisation for Economic Cooperation and Development (2006d) *Starting Strong II: Early Childhood Education and Care*. Paris: OECD Publishing, Annexe E – Germany, pp. 333–41.

Pascall, G. (1986) *Social Policy: A Feminist Analysis*. London: Tavistock, p. 38, quoted in A. Kelly (2004) 'Child health', cited in T. Maynard and N. Thomas (2008) *An Introduction to Early Childhood Studies*. London: Sage, p. 171.

Paton, G. (2007) 'Policy and practice in Scottish early childhood centres', *European Early Childhood Education Research*, 15 (3): 441–54.

Peeters, J. (2008) *The Construction of a New Profession: A European Perspective on Professionalism in Early Childhood Education and Care*. Amsterdam: SWP Publishers.

Powell, J. (2007) 'Multi-agency development and issues of communication', in A.D. Nurse (ed) (2007) *The New Early Years Professional: Dilemmas and Debates*. Oxford: Routledge, p.27.

Press, F. (2007) 'Public investment, fragmentation and quality in early education and care: existing challenges and future options', in C. Woodrow (2008) 'Discourse of professional identity in early childhood: movements in Australia', *European Early Childhood Education Research*, 16(2): 269–80.

Pugh, G. (2007) 'The policy agenda for Early Years services', in G. Pugh and B. Duffy (eds), *Contemporary Issues in the Early Years,* 4th edn. London: Sage, p. 17.

Pugh, G. and Duffy, B. (eds) (2007) *Contemporary Issues in the Early Years,* 4th edn. London: Sage, p. 18.

Quinton, D. (2004) *Supporting Parents: Messages form Research*. London. Jessica Kingsley.

Reggio Children Exhibition Catalogue (1996) *I Cento Linguaggi dei Bambini/The Hundred Languages of Children*. Reggio Emilia, Italy.

Rinaldi, C. and Spaggiari, S. (1996) *The Hundred Languages of Children*. Reggio Milia: Reggio Children, p. 215.

Rodd, J. (1997) 'Learning to be leaders: perceptions of early childhood professionals about leadership roles and responsibilities', *Early Years*, 18(1): 40–6.

Rummery, K. (2003) 'Social work and multi-disciplinary collaboration in primary health care', in J. Weinstein, C. Whittington and T. Leiba (eds), *Collaboration in Social Practice*. London: Jessica Kingsley, pp. 201–17.

Sanders, B. (2008) 'Interagency and multidisciplinary working', in T. Maynard and N. Thomas (2008) *An Introduction to Early Childhood Studies*. London: Sage, p. 186.

Schweinhart, L. J. (2004) *The HighScope Perry Preschool Study Through Age 40: Summary, Conclusions, and Frequently Asked Questions*. Ypsilanti, MI: HighScope Press.

Schweinhart, L. J., Barnes, H. V., Weikart, D. P. (1993) *Significant Benefits: The HighScope Perry Preschool Study Through Age 27*. Ypsilanti, MI: HighScope Press.

Shor, I. (1992) *Empowering Education*. London: University of Chicago Press.

Siraj-Blatchford, I., Clarke, K. and Needham, M. (2008) *The Team Around the Child: Multiagency Working in the Early Years*. Nottingham: Trentham Books.

Siraj-Blatchford, I., Milton, E., Sylva, K., Laugharne, J. and Charles, F. (2007) 'Developing the Foundation Phase for 3–7 year-olds in Wales', *Welsh Journal of Education*, 14 (1): 43–68.

Stephen, C. (2006) *Early Years Education: Perspectives from a Review of the International Literature*. Scottish Government Publications; available online at: www.scotland.gov.uk/Publications/2006/02/06145130/8.

Taba, S., Castle, A., Vermeer, M., Hanchett, K., Flores, D. and Caulfield, R. (1999) 'Lighting the path: developing leadership in early education', *Early Childhood Education*, 26 (3): 173–7.

Thomas, N. (2004) 'Law relating to children', in T. Maynard and N. Thomas, *An Introduction to Early Childhood Studies*, 3rd edn. London: Sage, pp. 109ff.

United Nations Children's Fund (2005) *The State of the World's Children*, cited in OECD (2006) *Starting Strong II: Early Childhood Education and Care*. Paris: OECD Publishing.

Waller, T. (2009) 'International perspectives', in M. Clark and T. Waller, *An Introduction to Early Childhood*, 2nd edn. London: Sage, p. 104.

Waniganayake, M., Morda, R. and Kapsalakis, A. (2000) 'Leadership in child care centres: is it just another job?', *Australian Journal of Early Childhood*, 25(1): 13–19.

Weinstein, J., Whittington, C. and Leiba, T. (eds) (2003) *Collaboration in Social Practice*. London: Jessica Kingsley.

Whalley, M. and the Pen Green Centre Team (2007) *Involving Parents in their Children's Learning*, 2nd edn. London: Paul Chapman.

Whalley, M., Chandler, R., John, K., Reid, L., Thorpe, S. and Everitt, J. (2008) 'Developing and sustaining leadership learning communities: implications of NPQICL rollout for public policy local praxis', *European Early Childhood Education Research*, 16(1): 5–38.

Whitaker, P. (1998) *Managing Schools*. Oxford: Butterworth Heinemann, cited in the NPQICL Participant Handbook (2004) *Leadership Concepts and Analytical Tools*, NCSL, p. 28.

Whittington, C., cited in J. Weinstein, C. Whittington and T. Leiba (eds) (2003) *Collaboration in Social Practice*. London: Jessica Kingsley, pp. 48–50.

Woodrow, C. (2008) 'Discourses of professional identity in early childhood: movements in Australia', *European Early Childhood Education Research*, 16(2): 269–80.

Woodrow, C. and Bush, G. (2008) 'Repositioning early childhood leadership as action and activism', *European Early Childhood Education Research*, 16(1): 83–94.

Index

Note: the letter 'f' after a page number refers to a figure; the letter 't' refers to a table.